The Trial and of John Church

The Preacher of the Surrey Tabernacle, Borough Road, at the Surrey Assizes, at Croydon, on Saturday, the 16th of August, 1817, for an Assault With Intent to Commit an Unnatural Crime.

Anonymous

Alpha Editions

This edition published in 2024

ISBN : 9789362095206

Design and Setting By
Alpha Editions
www.alphaedis.com
Email - info@alphaedis.com

As per information held with us this book is in Public Domain.
This book is a reproduction of an important historical work. Alpha Editions uses the best technology to reproduce historical work in the same manner it was first published to preserve its original nature. Any marks or number seen are left intentionally to preserve its true form.

Contents

TO THE PUBLIC. ....- 1 -
THE TRIAL, &C. &C. ....- 4 -
THE KING VERSUS JOHN CHURCH. ....- 4 -
Adam Foreman, the first witness was then called and examined by Mr. BOLLAND. ....- 8 -
THOMAS WEST was next sworn. ....- 17 -
DEFENCE. ....- 29 -
THE CHARGE. ....- 46 -

TO THE PUBLIC.

IN presenting to you the following account of the Trial of JOHN CHURCH, for an attempt to commit one of the foulest crimes recognized by the law of nature, the Publishers have no wish to echo the triumphs of a party—they are actuated only with a desire to hold up the abominable wretch to general observation, that innocent youths may not unguardedly become the victims of his brutal passion—the occasion calls for sorrow rather than joy; and the Christian Philanthropist will feel more inclined to shed the silent tear, than indulge in exultation, while he peruses this record of human degradation.

In some cases, it appears desirable not to suffer trials of a criminal nature to appear in print, particularly when the facts are too indecent, lest the tender feelings of any should be injured, or that information given which had better be withheld; but when the subject of conviction is a creature, who pretends to be the guide of hundreds in the paths of our Holy Religion, and under its sacred name, is not only ruining the bodies, but the souls of many of his hearers, than silence becomes a crime, and a full exposure an imperative duty.

We regret, that among the followers of this wretch are to be found many young men, who not only countenance his cause by their presence, but advocate it with their talents;—that charity, which covereth a multitude of sins, leads us to indulge the hope, that hitherto they have acted conscientiously and from principle—that they have believed their leader was the object of cruel persecution—that he suffered for righteousness sake—and under this impression, we pity rather than condemn them; but can they be of the same opinion now? We request their attentive perusal of the following pages; we beg of them to notice the evidence produced for the prosecution, particularly the copy of a letter to Mrs. Hunter, the original of which was artfully suppressed, and the admission of Church himself, and then say, whether this *conviction* does not *"confirm ancient reports?"* Let them read the contradictory evidence of Thomas, and the observations made thereon by the learned Judge who tried the prisoner; let those who were present remember his agitated appearance in Court, and the manner in which he unwillingly confirmed the evidence of the prosecutor's master, and then say on which side the *truth* appears to preponderate. If the hearers of Church do not wilfully close their eyes, and pervert their judgments, they can have but one opinion, viz. that the verdict of the jury is the verdict of every one who values the cause of religion, morality, and virtue.

If however, the hearers of this creature still continue to frequent this "Tabernacle of Iniquity," every person will naturally believe, that other motives, and not a desire to be edified by the ministrations of their *convicted* pastor, actuate them—they will ever be looked upon with a suspicious eye, and their character, and every thing that is dear to them in this life, will be sacrificed for ever, in the opinion of every good man.

It may be expected that something should be said of the conduct of those females who have so long patronized this deceiver of their souls. How can they longer listen to a wretch who must *detest* them in his heart, and nothing but his love of gain makes him court their friendship? Can they now, in the presence of a disgusted public, enter the doors of his "den of thieves?"—If they can, friends must blush for the inconsistency of their conduct: most sincerely do we hope that all who respect their reputation will never approach "the Surrey Tabernacle" until the present occupier and all his associates have left the place.

Much praise is due to those who have at last brought JOHN CHURCH to justice: every thing that could be done by bribery and persuasion were resorted to by his friends; but they found the Prosecutor, in this respect, invulnerable. The youth has acted nobly; and the praises of the Public are due to him for his resistance to the wishes of that wretch, who would have gloried in being the murderer of his peace for ever!

One fact however, as it reflects considerable *credit* on the *respectability* of the Defendant and his legal friend, must not be omitted—the person employed to *defend* the Prisoner was a Jew Attorney, very well known to many. He applied to the Prosecutor's father several times, and tendered his services to conduct the prosecution, assuring him he should not expect any pecuniary remuneration for his exertions in bringing such a character to justice. He advised the Father, as he was a poor man, to accept a sum of money, if it were offered, and compromise the business: this proposal was indignantly rejected, and the man treated as he deserved to be—with merited contempt. We regret also that a man, whose duty is the apprehension of transgressors against our laws, should have interfered most unjustly to hush up the matter.

Some, perhaps, may think that too much severity appears in our observations against the Prisoner—but, can this be the case? Can any man feel too indignant at the conduct of such miscreants?—We cordially agree with the learned Counsel for the Prisoner, that if a wish would sweep such characters from the creation, that wish would be immediately expressed by every true British heart.—Are we too severe? *Remember the conduct of the Almighty, who sent fire and brimstone from Heaven, and consumed the GUILTY Inhabitants of Sodom and Gomorrah, lest their filthy bodies should pollute the grave.*

The friends of the Prisoner have publicly supported him in his defence by their Subscriptions. The Prosecutor has stood almost alone; but, confident that the liberality of the Public was never appealed to in vain—that they will always assist the injured poor in bringing their oppressors to punishment, this Publication is submitted to them; and they may rest assured that the profits will be devoted towards defraying the expenses which have been necessarily incurred in bringing this "Monster of Iniquity" to Justice.

21st August, 1817.

THE TRIAL, &C. &C.

THE KING VERSUS JOHN CHURCH.

THE Indictment charged, "That the Defendant, late of the parish of St. Mary, Lambeth, in the county of Surrey, on the 26th day of September, in the fifty-seventh year of the reign of George the Third, with force and arms, at the parish aforesaid, in the county aforesaid, in and upon one Adam Foreman, in the peace of God and our said Lord the King, then and there being, did make an assault, and him, the said Adam Foreman, then and there did beat, wound, and ill treat, so that his life was greatly despaired of, with intent, that most horrid, detestable, and sodomitical crime (among Christians not to be named) called Buggery, with the said Adam Foreman, against the order of nature, then, and there feloniously, wickedly, and devilishly, to commit and do, to the great displeasure of Almighty God, to the great damage of the said Adam Foreman, and against the peace." &c.

The second count charged a common assault.

The Defendant pleaded—NOT GUILTY.

Counsel for the Prosecution—Mr. MARRYATT and Mr. BORLAND; Solicitor, Mr. HARMER.

Counsel for the Defendant—Mr. GURNEY and the COMMON SERJEANT.

The Jury being sworn:—Mr. BORLAND opened the indictment, as follows—

May it please your Lordship, Gentlemen of the Jury—The Defendant, John Church, stands indicted for a misdemeanour. He has pleaded Not Guilty, and your charge is to enquire whether he be Guilty or Not Guilty. Hearken to the evidence.

Mr. MARRYATT then stated the case on the part of the Prosecution, to the effect following:—

May it please your Lordship, Gentlemen of the Jury—I am extremely sorry to have occasion to state to you that the offence imputed to the Defendant (which my Learned Friend, Mr. Bolland; simply opened as a misdemeanour) is an assault, with the intent to commit an unnatural crime; and I am sure, on an occasion of this nature, it would be unnecessary for me to bespeak your serious attention to a charge so serious in its consequences to the Defendant. The Prosecutor in this case is a youth, about eighteen or nineteen years of age, the apprentice of a Potter at Vauxhall, whose name is Patrick. He had been apprenticed to him some time, and resided in his family. The Defendant is a preacher—not of the Established Church, but of a Dissenting Chapel, not far distant from Vauxhall, and Mr. Patrick and his family had been in the habit of attending that Chapel and hearing Mr.

Church's discourses. Their apprentice used frequently to accompany them to the Chapel, and by that means he became perfectly acquainted with the person and voice of the Defendant, Church. He knew him extremely well by name and description. In the month of September last, Mr. Church complained to Mr. Patrick that he was in ill health, and attributed that circumstance to the confined situation of his apartments near to the Chapel. Being ill, Mr. Patrick, as a matter of civility and attention to the Preacher of the Chapel which he frequented, invited him to come to Vauxhall, where he had a spare bed, much at Mr. Church's service. Upon this invitation, Mr. Church came, and he slept there on Monday, the 23d of September, for the first time. I am not quite certain as to the precise night he came; but on the night of the 26th day of September, the transaction occurred which gave rise to the present proceeding. Mr. Patrick had left town on business, but not before Mr. Church came in the first instance; but during Church's stay he departed for the country. During the master's absence, it became necessary for Foreman, the apprentice, to sleep in the house. The only spare bed was occupied by Church, the Defendant, and therefore a temporary bed was made up for the apprentice. He had a resting place made up for him in one of the parlours of the house. It happened that on the evening when this transaction took place, the Prosecutor had been staying up to attend a kiln which was at work on Mr. Patrick's premises.

Mr. GURNEY.—I am told one of your witnesses is now in Court.

Mr. MARRYATT.—I am not aware of that circumstance. If he is, he must certainly go out of Court.

Mr. GURNEY.—I am told Mr. Patrick is in Court.

Mr. MARRYATT.—Then I beg he will go out; and that all the witnesses will remain outside until they are severally called.

Gentlemen, I was stating to you, that on the night in question, Mr. Patrick went out of town on some business. An occasional bed was made up for the apprentice. Mr. Church occupied the only spare bed-room in the house. The apprentice, I believe, was not in the habit of sleeping in Mr. Patrick's family, except when his master went out of town; for otherwise there would be no occasion to make up a temporary bed for him, if he was in the practice of sleeping there. Between twelve and one o'clock in the morning, the apprentice retired from the burning of the kiln, to take his rest in the bed thus assigned him. He got into bed, and went to sleep almost immediately; and at no very great distance of time, he was awakened by the approach of Mr. Church in his bed-room. Mr. Church was not ignorant where the young man slept and the manner in which he was accommodated. The apprentice was alarmed, and certainly had no doubt of what Mr. Church's intention was in coming to his bed-chamber. You must hear the circumstances from the witness; and I have very little doubt that you will be satisfied from his evidence, and that of the other witnesses I shall have to call, that the intention of the defendant was that imputed to him by this indictment. The advances and overtures made to the apprentice in the way that he will describe to you, must leave very little doubt in your mind of the intention of the person who went into that room. Indeed it would be very difficult to assign any good reason for Mr. Church's coming there. The lad was surprised. He awoke and laid hold of the person by the arm, and called out, "Who is there?" The Defendant said, in a feigned feminine voice, "Don't you know me, Adam? I'm your mistress."—The lad was extremely surprised at this; he knew that it was not his mistresses voice; and he knew by having caught hold of the shirt sleeve of the person who addressed him, that it was not a woman, but a man. In consequence of this, he endeavoured to lay hold of him; the Defendant however retired from the room and went up stairs. I told you that the lad had a temporary bed made up for him in the parlour; and upon the defendant's retiring from the room, the prosecutor had a distinct opportunity of seeing his person; for it seems that the door of the parlour was opposite the fan-light over the street door, through which a light was given by the lamp in the street; and upon the Defendant's retiring, the prosecutor had a distinct view of him, and knew him extremely well to be Mr. Church. He hardly knew how to act. He was unwilling to alarm his mistress at that hour of the night; not indeed that it was a story fit to be mentioned, or stated to her at any time by him. He, however, went out of the house to the person whom he had left at the kiln in the pottery when he retired to rest. That person's name is West; and he gave him an account of what had passed. West was for going into the house and turning the Defendant Church immediately out; but the prosecutor said it would occasion an alarm to his mistress, and he thought it better to postpone the business until the morning. Accordingly, Mr. Church was not disturbed for that night; but in the morning some inquiry was made by Mrs. Patrick, who asked whether the prosecutor and the servants had not been disturbed in the course of the night, by some persons coming up or down stairs? Some explanation was given her of the cause of the disturbance, but not to the full extent, it being thought adviseable not to explain the whole to her, as Mr. Patrick was returning home that night, when the prosecutor determined to detail the whole transaction to his master. The prosecutor had given his mistress some account of what had occurred, but withholding from her that part which he thought improper for female ears to hear. Mr. Patrick however came home the next day, and the prosecutor told his story to him; and on the following day several of Mr. Church's friends having heard that the boy had told his master what had occurred, came to Mr. Patrick to inquire what was the extent of the information he had received. Mr. Patrick communicated to them the whole of the information which the boy had given, and said he thought it necessary that Mr. Church should explain his conduct. By this time the thing was generally known and buzzed about. Some of the congregation were desirous that no proceeding should be instituted against the Defendant, as the public investigation of such a transaction would be a disgrace to the individuals of the congregation and to the cause of religion itself. Whilst Mr. Patrick and some of his friends, who were of the same religious persuasion, were some days hesitating about what course to pursue, the boy's father came to the knowledge of the transaction; and he without any sort of ceremony took him before a Magistrate and laid the complaint which has given rise to this prosecution against the Defendant, Mr. Church.

Much inquiry has since taken place; and the Defendant has endeavoured to explain; the transaction as well as he could; and he has written various letters upon the subject. Those letters are here, and they are much at Mr. Church's service if he thinks there is any thing contained in them which will afford him any defence; because I do not think it right to withhold any thing which can throw light upon such a transaction.

Amongst other things which Mr. Church urged by way of explanation, in these letters, was a contradiction of some of the particulars stated the prosecutor. He said, that there were some matters in the statement of the boy which he was able to contradict. This declaration of Mr. Church having come to the knowledge of Mr. Patrick, he was induced by the application which was made to him, on the part of some of Mr. Church's congregation, to make some inquiry of Mr. Church upon the subject. He accordingly took occasion to have an interview with the defendant, for the purpose of enabling himself, if he could, to explain his conduct to the satisfaction of the persons who are in the habit of attending his chapel. At that interview, he contradicted some of the particularities stated by the boy, but which are some of the most disgusting parts of the narrative. He, however, admitted, most distinctly, that he had gone into the lad's room.

Now, when you shall have had it proved in evidence, that part of the conduct ascribed to him was admitted by the defendant, I should like to know if he really did go into that bed-room, for what possible purpose could he go there in the middle of the night? It will appear, still further, that Church was the only male person who slept in the house; for there was no other individual of the male sex to take up his abode there that night.

The question, then, will be, whether, upon the evidence I shall produce, you can have any reasonable doubt of the defendant's intention to commit the offence imputed to him by this indictment? If you have no doubt of the truth of the boy's story—if you have no doubt that it was the defendant's intention to commit the atrocious crime charged upon him by this prosecution, then, however painful your duty may be, you must not be deterred by the enormity and apparent impossibility of such a crime existing in society, from the fair and honest discharge of it. There are two questions for you to determine:—*First*, whether the defendant was the person who entered the prosecutor's room?—and, *Secondly*, if he did, whether the atrocious intention, alleged in the indictment can clearly be inferred from his conduct on that occasion? But, gentlemen, if you have any reasonable doubt upon either of these questions, I should not, as Counsel for the prosecution, desire you to pronounce a verdict of guilty. But, whatever conclusion you may draw from his statement, submitted to your consideration, I trust you will take care that your indignation against the offence itself shall not carry you to the conclusion of guilt, unless the evidence I shall lay before you warrants the conviction of the defendant.

Adam Foreman, the first witness was then called and examined by Mr. BOLLAND.

How old are you?—I shall be twenty the first day of December next.

I believe you are an apprentice to Mr. Patrick, the potter, of Vauxhall?—Yes.

How long have you been with him?—About five years.

Do you know the defendant, John Church?—Yes, by sight.

How long have you known him?—About two or three years.

What is he?—A preacher.

Have you attended the congregation in the Chapel where he preaches?—Yes.

And have you often seen him?—Oh, yes.

Do you sleep generally at your masters house, or at your fathers?—At my father's generally.

Are there any occasions upon which you do sleep at your master's house?—Yes.

When is that?—When he goes out of town.

When your master goes out of town, then you sleep at his house?—Yes.

Where did Church reside? Where did he live?—He lived by his chapel.

Where is that?—In St. George's Fields. It comes out of the Borough-road.

There he lived?—Yes.

Now, did he at any time come to take up his abode at Mr. Patrick's?—Yes.

When was that?—The 25th of September, he came to sleep there that night.

Do you know what was the occasion of his coming?

Mr. GURNEY.—That must be of his own knowledge.

Mr. BOLLAND.—Mr. Patrick will tell us.—I believe he came—

Mr. GURNEY.—You must not tell us, Sir, unless you know it of your own knowledge.

However, he came to sleep there?—Yes.

Did you sleep there that night?—Yes.

Was that the first night he came?—I don't know whether he had been there before. I cannot say whether I had seen him there before.

You know that he slept there on the 25th of September, and that you were there?—Yes.

Where was your master that night?—He was out of town; but where, I cannot say.

Who slept in the house that night?—Mr. Church, my mistress, the children, and the two maid servants.

Was there any other man in the house, except yourself and Church?—No.

Where was your bed room?—The front parlour on the first floor.

That is the ground floor?—It is over the kitchen.

Is that a bed-room in common in the house?—No, it is not.

Then how came you to sleep there?—Because there was not any other bedroom that I could sleep in.

Was a temporary bed therefore put up for you there?—Yes.

Now, at what time did you retire to rest?—Near one o'clock.

What had kept you up so late?—There was a kiln burning, and I was obliged to sit up to let the man into the kiln when he came.

Was it necessary for you to sit up to attend that kiln?—Yes; and to give the key to the man.

Who was that man?—Thomas West.

And you went to bed about one o'clock?—Yes.

Did you go to sleep?—Yes; directly I went to bed.

After you had been asleep, did any thing happen to you?—Yes.

State what it was?—I had not been asleep more than half an hour, before I was awoke by some one putting his hands under the bed clothes, and laying hold of my private parts.

In what way?—Laid hold of me very tight.

Did you say any thing, or did the person, whoever it was, say any thing to you?—Yes. I put my hand out of the bed clothes, and caught hold of him, and asked him who he was?

What did you say?—I asked him who he was—I said who are you?

And you say you laid hold of him?—Yes.

By what part did you lay hold of him?—As near as I can guess it was the upper part of his arm.

Upon laying hold of him, what observation did you make? What did you ascertain from laying hold of the person? Could you tell whether it was a man or a woman?—I laid hold of his arm, and felt lower down, and found by the sleeve that he had got a man's shirt on.

How far did you feel lower down?—I had a hold of him by the upper part of the arm, and running my hand down to the wrist, I found he had a man's shirt on.

Could you tell whether the wrist was buttoned?—Yes.

Was it buttoned?—It was.

Could you tell at all by the feel of the arm itself, whether it was the arm of a man or a woman?—I knew very well it was a man.

Could you tell that from the feel of the flesh?—I could not tell that.

By Lord ELLENBOROUGH.—You knew it was a man—By what circumstance?—Because he had got a man's shirt on.

You knew it was a man by the shirt?—Yes.

By Mr. BOLLAND.—Did the person say any thing to you in answer to what you said?—He answered—"Adam, don't you know me? I am your mistress," in a faint voice, like a woman.

And was it the voice of your mistress, Mrs. Patrick?—Oh! no, sir!

Could you tell whose voice it was?—Yes; I knew the voice directly I heard it.

Whose voice was it?—Mr. Church's.

What did you do afterwards, and what did he do?—He fled from the room directly.

When you use the word *fled*, what do you mean by that?—He went out of the room.

The word *fled* indicates more than merely going out of the room; did he go out in a hurried manner?—He went out in a hurried step.

Upon his going out what did you do?—I got out of bed, and put on my small clothes and shoes, and went to the man up at the kiln.

What did you do first—when he went out of the room—what did you first do?—I got out of bed, and put on my small clothes and shoes.

Did you see him go out of the room?—Yes. As he opened the door I saw by the lamp that it was Mr. Church, and he had only his shirt on.

Where is that lamp that enabled you to see the person of Church?—Outside of the door.

What door do you mean?—Outside of the front street door.

In the street?—Yes; on the Terrace.

And that lamp throws a light through the fan-light of the hall door?—Yes.

By Lord ELLENBOROUGH.—The lamp is at the street door?—Yes, my Lord.

By Mr. BOLLAND.—Is it a gas light or a parish light?—It is a parish lamp.

It is not one of the new lights?—No.

It is not a gas light?—No.

By Lord ELLENBOROUGH.—Where were you standing at the time?—I was getting up, my Lord.

By Mr. BOLLAND.—Did you go out of your room?—Yes, I did.

By Lord ELLENBOROUGH.—You say that when he went out of the room, you saw it was Church, by the lamp: what lamp do you mean?—The lamp at the door.

What door?—The street door.

Where were you when you saw Church at that time by the light of the lamp?—In bed, sitting up. I had not then left my bed.

You must have opened your door?—No, my Lord; Church did that.

By Mr. BOLLAND.—Whoever the person was, he left the door open, and you saw him go out through that door; and then you observed that he had a shirt on?—Yes.

The shirt or dress of a man is much shorter than that of a woman, and therefore you must have seen whether it was a shirt or a shift?—It was the shirt of a man, I am sure.

Did you see his face at all?—No, I did not. His back was to me.

When he was gone, what did you do?—I then got up and put my small clothes on, and shoes, and went into the pottery.

What for?—To get the man to come up to the house.

Did you inform any body of what had happened?—Yes; I told Thomas West of it.

By LORD ELLENBOROUGH.—He was in the pottery?—Yes.

By Mr. BOLLAND.—Was that the Thomas West that was in the pottery before you went to bed?—Yes.

Cross-examined by Mr. GURNEY.

The person, whoever it was, you say left the door open behind him?—No; he opened the door and went out.

Did he shut the door after him?—Yes.

Is that so?—Yes.

Then, if he shut the door after him, how did that enable you to see any thing by the light?—When he opened the door I saw him.

There was no light in the room?—No.

The light, as you say, came from a lamp on the Terrace?—Yes.

How far is that lamp from the door?—Between five and six yards from the door on the Terrace.

The Terrace on which your master's house is situated, is a row of houses raised above the road?—Yes.

And the lamp is upon the Terrace opposite the door.—Yes.

And about five or six yards from the door?—Yes.

The light which it given to your passage is, I suppose, through the fan-light over the door?—Yes.

Then you mean to say that the light which came through that fan-light into your passage enabled you to see who it was, before the person had left the room?—When he opened the door and went out I saw him.

You say that the person, whoever he was, shut the door immediately afterwards?—Yes; but I could see him when he opened the door.

Did you see the face of the person?—No.

How then can you pretend to say that you knew who that person was?—I saw that the person had a shirt on.

Do you mean to say that you can distinguish a shirt from a shift or a bed-gown?—I saw that it was a shirt.

I should imagine that on an occasion of this sort you were a little frightened?—Yes, I was rather alarmed.

Waked out of your sleep in this way, you were of course rather alarmed.—Did it not take place all in a minute?—Yes, it was not long about.

Did it not take place almost instantaneously?—I don't know how long he had been there before I awoke.

From the moment you awoke, did it not take place as fast as possible?—Yes.

Now, you say you went directly to West?—Yes.

West and you directly came and searched the house for thieves?—Yes. We did not know whether any body had got in or not.

And went and looked at every chamber door in the house?—Yes; except Mr. Church's and my mistress's.

Did you not look at the door of Mr. Church and that of your mistress?—Yes; but we did not open them.

I suppose therefore they were both of them shut?—Yes.

Did you find any door open?—No.

You looked at all the doors in the house and found them all shut?—Yes; the servant's door was on the jar.

You mean the maid servant's door?—Yes.

The other doors of the house were all shut?—All the other doors were shut.

And after you and he searched the house all over, you went to bed and he went back to the pottery?—No; he stopped while I put on the remainder of my clothes, and I went back with him to the pottery, after having locked the door.

You went with him to the pottery?—Yes.

And you say that you told West this story directly?—Yes, I told him that Mr. Church came down into my room and behaved in a very indecent manner.

You told him, I take for granted, that Church had been there, and laid hold of your private parts?—Yes.

You told him that Mr. Church had laid hold of your private parts?—Yes.

How came that to be a reason for you and be searching the house for thieves?—I did not search the house for thieves in particular; but to search if any body was in any of the rooms.

But I asked you before whether you did not search the house for thieves; and you answered "Yes."—Are you right or wrong in that?—I asked you before whether you and he did not search the house for thieves, and you told me that you did?—We searched the house: we looked all over it, to see if there was any body in any of the rooms.

And therefore I asked you expressly whether you and he did not search the house for thieves? and did you not say expressly that you and he had searched the house for thieves?—We searched the house; but not for thieves in particular.

Then you did not think of thieves?—I did not think of thieves, because I knew who it was.

You did not go into the maid servant's room?—No, we looked in.

You did not go in?—No; we found the door open, and looked in.

They were, of course, in bed?—Yes; one was my sister.

Lord ELLENBOROUGH.—Did the two maids sleep in that room?—Yes, my Lord; one is my sister.

Mr. GURNEY.—The door being ajar, you pushed it in a little, and you saw they were abed?—Yes.

Lord ELLENBOROUGH.—Did you speak to them?—No.

Re-examined by Mr. BOLLARD.

You say you did not search the house for thieves?—No; not for thieves.

Because you knew who the person was?—Yes.

Was the reason of your searching the house because you wished to be quite right before you made the accusation against Mr. Church?—Yes.

And you found that there was no other man in the house?—We found there was no other man in the house but Mr. Church.

Was there any door or window open at which any other man could have come in?—No.

Now this light from the terrace, did that strike through the fan-light or window over the door?—Yes.

Does it give a pretty fair light to the hall?—Yes; it shews a little light up the stairs.

And at the time the person opened the door and went out, was it at that time you got this view of his person?—Yes.

Examined by Lord ELLENBOROUGH.

Now, you say that he came into the room—Did you hear him when he first came into the room?—No.

You were awakened, as I understand you, by the application of his hand to your person?—Yes.

Was he on the bed, or standing by the side of the bed on the floor?—He was standing upon the floor.

When he assumed a feigned voice, and said, "I am your mistress," and when you observed it to be a feigned voice in which he was speaking, did you not speak to him by name, and say, "It is you, Mr. Church"—(*The Witness seemed to hesitate, as if he had not understood the question*)—Have you any difficulty in hearing?—No, my Lord.

You did not call to him by name, or give him to understand that you knew who he was?—No.

Did you see any part of his person or any part of his face from which you knew, in addition to the knowledge you derived at hearing his voice, that it was the Defendant, Church?—Yes, I did.

What part of his person did you see that led you to believe it was Mr. Church?—I saw his back as he went out of the room.

Did it appear to be the height of Mr. Church?—Yes.

What height is he?—I cannot say.

What had he upon his head: had he a night-cap?—He had a night-cap.

Was it a man's night-cap?—I cannot exactly say whether it was or no; I think it was a handkerchief tied round his head.

What sort of a handkerchief was it; was it a coloured handkerchief?—I could not tell that.

When you and West searched the house and examined the different doors, did you go to Mr. Church's door?—Yes; but we did not touch it, nor did we go in.

Why did you not call to Mr. Church; and, as you were with West, why did you not require that Mr. Church should appear, in order that you might, by an immediate view, ascertain whether he was the person who had entered your room, and acted in the way you have described?—West wanted to go into the room and pull him out.

Then, when West wanted to pull him out, why did you not, at least, call to him?—Because I was afraid of disturbing my mistress; she would have been very much alarmed.

Had he ever any conversation with you, or did he ever make any overture of this sort to you before this time?—No, my Lord.

There was nothing particular in his manner or in his conduct towards you before this time?—No, my Lord.

There was nothing particular in his manner or conduct towards you before this time?—No.

How soon did you see him after this to speak to him?—I have not spoken to him at all since.

Have you never spoken to him since?—No, my Lord.

Has he not attended before a Magistrate with you?—Yes.

There you spoke in his presence, but not immediately to him?—I spoke in his presence, but not to him.

Upon hearing him at the Office before the Magistrate, did that confirm the opinion you entertained of his being the person who entered your room?—I did not hear him speak before the Magistrate.

You did not hear him speak before the Magistrate?—He did not speak at all before the Magistrate.

Did you give the same account before the Magistrate that you have now done here?—Yes, my Lord.

You do not know whether it was a handkerchief or a night-cap that was upon his head?—I don't know whether it was a handkerchief or a night-cap.

Are there any other circumstances from which you could collect that it was a man?—No, my Lord.

Did the hand continue upon your person for any length of time, and for how long?—Not after I waked at all.

The hand was withdrawn then?—Yes.

And did the person say any thing to you?—He said that he was my mistress.

By the height of the person you saw, you could ascertain whether it was or was not the height of your mistress, or any of the female part of the house?—Yes; Mr. Church was a great deal bigger than any body there.

What is the size of Mr. Church?—I don't think he is quite six foot to my knowledge.

Is he a tall man or a short man?—He is a tallish stout man.

Was there light enough by the lamp that you have spoken of to see the outline of the man so as to be able to say that he was a tall person?—Yes.

What sort of a person is Mrs. Patrick?—She is a very little woman.

Quite a different person from the person you saw in the room?—O yes, my Lord, quite so.

The maid, who slept in the room with your sister, what was her person and size?—She was about at tall as I am—(*The Witness was about five feet seven*)—not quite so tall.

You are sure it was not her?—O yes, my Lord.—*The Witness withdrew.*

THOMAS WEST was next sworn.

Examined by Mr. MARRYATT.

Are you workman to Mr. Patrick, the Potter?—Yes.

Did you, on the morning of the 26th September last relieve Adam Foreman at the kiln?—I did.

About what time of that morning did you relieve him?—About half-past twelve o'clock.

You went to the Pottery to relieve him?—Yes.

Did he leave you shortly afterwards for the purpose of going to bed?—Yes, he did.

How long had he left you before you saw him again?—About an hour.

When you saw him again, was he dressed or only part dressed?—Only part.

What part of his dress had he on?—He had his small-clothes, his shoes, and one stocking.

When he came to you in that condition, did he state to you any thing that had passed since he left you?—He came to me in a very great fright, and bid me light my candle; he appeared very much alarmed, and bid me light my candle, and come along with him.

Where were you to go with him?—Up to the house.

What did he state to you that had passed?—He told me, as we were going along the garden, that Mr. Church had been to him and behaved in a very indecent manner.

Did he explain how?—No, he did not.

Did you go into the house with him?—Yes; he unlocked the door, and we went in.

The door of what?—The back door, where we went into the house.

The outer door?—Yes.

The garden door?—Yes.

When you got to the house, what did you and he do?—He went and put the remainder of his clothes on.

Well; what did you and he do?—We went and searched every room in the house, beginning at the bottom, and going on upwards to the top, except my mistress's room and Mr. Church's.

Did you go into all the other rooms; did you open them all?—We went into all the rooms except Mr. Church's and Mrs. Patrick's.

You did not go into Mr. Church's room, or into that of your mistress?—No.

Did you open the doors of those two rooms?—We did not open the door of either of those two rooms.

When you came to Mr. Church's door, did you say any thing?—Yes; I said, "I'll go and pull him out; shall I?" The lad said, "No," for fear of disturbing his mistress.

Upon that observation of the lad's about disturbing his mistress, did you forbear going into the room?—Yes, I did.

What became of Foreman for the rest of the night?—He came along with me into the Pottery; he came down stairs, locked the back door, and staid with me the whole of the remainder of the night; he returned with me to the Pottery, and staid 'til the morning.

Now, for what purpose did you search in all the rooms of the house?—To see if there was any other person in the place.

Did you find any window or door open, at which any body could have got into the house?—No; I saw them all close and fastened.

Cross-examined by the COMMON SERJEANT.

When he came to you, he told you that Mr. Church had been there; but did not explain what he had done?—No.

That you are quite sure of?—Yes.

Lord ELLENBOROUGH.—What words did he use?—He only told me that Church had behaved in a very indecent manner to him.

COMMON SERJEANT.—You had never any intimation that there were thieves in the house? You did not go to search for thieves in the house?—When he told me that Church behaved in a very indecent manner to him, I went to see if there was any other person in the place.

Did he not tell you he believed there were thieves in the house?—No.

Lord ELLENBOROUGH.—I think you are misled by what the witness, Foreman, said. It is a mere form of expression. You are going upon a wrong scent. The witness did not say, in terms, that he believed there were thieves in the house.

COMMON SERJEANT.—That was particularly mentioned by Foreman in his examination.

Lord ELLENBOROUGH.—He might have used the word thieves; but it is very unimportant. It is giving a consequence to a phraze that is in very common use, and means very little.

Mr. GURNEY.—I put the question to him in terms, whether he did not go to search for thieves in the house.

Mr. MARRYATT.—He adopted the whole of the sentence certainly, in the answer he gave to the question.

Mr. BOLLAND.—There were two propositions in the question, which was, whether West and the witness did not go directly in search of thieves? and the answer applied to the first part of the question—"as to going together."

Lord ELLENBOROUGH.—It is a very common expression, and no consequence ought to be attached to it.

Mr. GURNEY.—We had heard before that he had made use of that phrase, and therefore we were desirous of questioning him about it.

COMMON SERJEANT.—You are quite sure he did not explain in what way this man behaved to him?—No.

Did he say any thing like this:—"That he came to his bed-side, and laid his hand upon his private parts?"—No, Sir.

This was on the night of the 25th of September?—Yes.

You, I believe, afterwards went before the Magistrate, at the same time with Foreman the apprentice?—Yes.

To Union Hall?—Yes.

Lord ELLENBOROUGH.—Did he not in the course of the morning, when staying with you, and after you had been to the house, tell you what Church had done to him, and that he had laid his hand upon his private parts?—No.

Never, from first to last?—No.

COMMON SERJEANT.—Pray, at what time was it that you went before the Magistrate with this young man? Was it at all earlier than the 12th of November following?—I cannot say the day of the month.

Was it not six or seven weeks afterwards?—It was some time afterwards.

Was it not six or seven weeks after?—I believe it was.

Mr. MARRYATT.—Did the lad then go with his father?—Yes.

COMMON SERJEANT.—The lad generally slept at home at his father's?—Yes.

Now, how far was his father's off from his master's?—About a quarter of a mile.

Did he not sleep at his father's the next night?—The next but one he did.

And yet it was not till about six or seven weeks after that, you went to the justice?—No.

Lord ELLENBOROUGH.—Did you communicate with Mr. Patrick upon the subject before you went to the Justice.—No, my Lord.

Mr. Patrick *sworn*. *Examined by* Mr. BOLLAND.

You are a potter at Vauxhall?—Yes.

How long was the boy, Foreman, with you?—Ever since I have been in the pottery business, between five and six years.

Did he sleep in your house?—Only occasionally.

Upon what occasion is it that he does sleep in your house? Whenever I leave town; and then he has the key of the pottery, there being no other male in the house.

Were you absent from home on the 25th September last?—Yes.

Was the boy on that occasion to sleep in your house?—Yes.

Where had the bed been put up for him?—It was a chair-bed in the front parlour; a temporary bed for a nurse occasionally.

Do you know the defendant, John Church?—Yes.

What is he, and when did you become acquainted with him?—He is a Baptist preacher; and I first became acquainted with him when I came to Vauxhall.

Did you attend his chapel?—Yes.

And you so became acquainted with him?—Yes.

Where was his residence?—Adjoining the chapel.

Now, in the month of September, upon any occasion, and what, did he come to sleep at your house, and did you put a bed up for him?—Yes.

On what occasion was it?—He had complained of ill health occasionally; and thinking that he was ill, I asked him out of friendship to take a bed at my house, supposing that the air would be of service to him.

You live near the river?—No; not very close.

You say you were out from home on the 25th of September. When did you return?—On the evening of the 26th.

Upon your return, did the boy, Foreman, make any communication to you?—He did the next morning when I saw him. I returned on the evening of the 26th.

By Lord ELLENBOROUGH.—Then it was the day but one after, namely, the morning of the 27th that the boy made the communication to you?—Yes, my Lord.

By Mr. BOLLAND.—Did you see Foreman on the night of your return?—Not to speak with him.

But on the morning of the 27th he made the communication to you?—Yes.

Respecting this transaction?—Yes, respecting this transaction.

What did you do upon the boy's making that communication?—I told him I was extremely sorry for what had happened.

You need not tell us what you told him. Did you make it known?—I had many applications from the Congregation, to whom I made it known.

Did the communication come first from you, or did they apply to you for information?—In consequence of the information they had received from general report, they applied to me for authentic information.

Several of the Congregation made those applications?—Yes.

What request was made to you, and in consequence of that request was there any meeting upon the subject?—Yes.

Mr. GURNEY.—Unless Church was present, this cannot be received as evidence.

The COMMON SERJEANT.—And even if he was present I apprehend it cannot be received, unless it is evidence of a fact.

Lord ELLENBOROUGH.—It is no evidence of a fact; but in consequence of something said by the Congregation respecting this subject, the witness did something. The question may be put in that shape.

Mr. GURNEY.—If my learned Friend goes to that, I have no objection to that question.

Mr. BOLLAND.—I was going on to put that question, if I had not been stopt by my learned Friend.

By Mr. BOLLAND.—In consequence of applications made to you from the Congregation, did you go to the Defendant, Church?—I did.

What did you state to Church; and when did you go to him upon this subject?—I think it was on the 9th of October.

Had there not before that been a meeting of the Congregation, at which you were present?—No.

By Lord ELLENBOROUGH.—Did you take any steps between the 27th of September, to see Church, and the 9th of October, upon this subject?—No, my Lord.

That was the first communication you had with Church upon this subject?—Yes.

By Mr. BOLLAND.—What did you say to him, or he to you, upon your going to him?—He took it extremely kind of me in calling upon him. I told him he might take it as he pleased; that I did not come willingly, but that some of his Congregation thought that I ought to see him on the business.

By Lord ELLENBOROUGH.—Did he appear to be apprized of the subject before you began?—I cannot say that, my Lord, exactly. But I believe he was apprized from what afterwards occurred.

By Mr. BOLLAND.—What passed on that occasion between you and him?—I told him I waited upon him, having seen a letter wherein he denied three particular points of the boy's statement; and I wished to know what those points were.

You told him you had seen a letter that he had written upon the subject?—Yes.

By Lord ELLENBOROUGH.—You told him you had seen a letter upon the subject, in which he denied three particular points of the boy's statement?—Yes.

By Mr. BOLLAND.—What did he say to that?—He said that he denied having hold of the boy, or the boy having hold of him; or he, Church, saying, that he was the boy's mistress.

He denied the boy having hold of him, or that he, Church, having said that he was the boy's mistress?—Yes.

Did he say whether or not he was in the room?—He admitted that fact.

But denied the laying hold of the boy's private parts?—Yes. He denied the laying hold.

Did he state any reason for being in the room?—Not at all.

By Lord ELLENBOROUGH.—When you say that he admitted being in the room, will you, as far as you can, state the words: state what he said?—He said that he denied three particular points, two of which I have already named. The other was something that did not occur to me to be important, and which I did not take any notice of, and consequently I do not remember it. I told him that of these two points, that I have mentioned, the boy was positive, and I had no reason to doubt any thing that the boy had said, as I had never known him to tell a lie. He said that he was sorry for it, because that confirmed *ancient reports*. I told him it did so; and of course I told him that now I should believe all that I had heard heretofore; and I wished him a good morning.

Now did you see him at any time afterwards?—Not to speak to him.

By Lord ELLENBOROUGH.—You have seen him, but not spoken to him since?—I have not spoken to him since, my Lord.

By Mr. BOLLAND.—What letter was it that you had seen which you spoke to him about?—A letter dated the 6th of October, addressed to a Mrs. Hunter, I took an exact copy of it. Mr. Harmer has it.

Is that the copy? (*A paper put into the witness's hand.*)

Mr. GURNEY.—I cannot see how this can be evidence, until they prove the original to be destroyed.

Lord ELLENBOROUGH.—This is only *a provisional* question.

By Mr. BOLLAND.—Is that the copy?—Yes, it is an exact copy.

By Lord ELLENBOROUGH.—Did you read that copy of the letter to him?—No, my Lord, I had not the copy at that time.

By Mr. BORLAND.—What did you state to him respecting the letter?—I told him I wished to know what the three things were which he could deny, as asserted by the boy?

You don't recollect the third point?—No.

By Lord ELLENBOROUGH.—You say it is not material?—No, my Lord.

By Mr. BOLLAND.—And you say he admitted being in the room, but denied the laying hold?—Yes.

In what terms did he admit that he was in the room?—He said, "I was in the room; but I did not lay hold of the boy."

By LORD ELLENBOROUGH.—Did he say why he was in the room?—No, my Lord.

What did you do with the letter of the 6th of October?—I returned it to Mrs. Hunter.

From whom did you get it?—From Mrs. Hunter.

And to Mrs. Hunter you returned it?—Yes.

Cross-examined by Mr. GURNEY.

You mean to say that he said distinctly to you that he was in the room?—Yes.

Did you mention to any person after you had seen Mr. Church, that he was not implicated in the affair at all?—No.—That *I* said *he* was not implicated?—No! I never said any such thing.

Did you give any person an account of the conversation you had with him, and accompany that account with this observation, "He is not at all implicated"?—Never.

Not to any person?—No; not to any person.

Did any person go with you to Mr. Church?—Mr. Thomas went to the door with me.

Is he a friend of your's?—He is no friend of mine. I had only seen him at the door. It was *his* wife and mine that wished me to make the application to Mr. Church.

Then Mr. Thomas went with you as far as the door, but did not go in with you?—No.

Do you recollect having any conversation with Mr. Thomas, in which you told him what had taken place between you and Mr. Church?—I told him briefly what had transpired; it was very short what did transpire.

And you told Mr. Thomas what had transpired at the interview with Mr. Church, when you came out?—Yes.

Then did you tell Mr. Thomas that Mr. Church admitted having been in the room?—I think I did; but I am not very positive as to that point. I know I told him that Mr. Church said that he did not lay hold of the boy.

The question I wish to put to you is this—whether Mr. Thomas did not ask you this question, "Well, is there any thing against Mr. Church, or not?"—and whether you did not answer, "No, he is not at all implicated?"—I never made any such answer to him.

Neither that, nor any thing conveying that meaning?—Never.

By LORD ELLENBOROUGH.—You never did tell him, directly or indirectly, that there was nothing to implicate Mr. Church?—No, never.

By Mr. GURNEY.—Did you either tell Mr. Thomas, or any other person that you would prosecute Mr. Church, because he had said disgraceful things of your wife?—I did; but not for this crime, but for defamation of my wife's character.

By LORD ELLENBOROUGH.—You told Mr. Thomas that you intended to prosecute Mr. Church for defaming your wife's character?—I don't know that I ever told Mr. Thomas; but I believe I have said that, or words to that effect, to other persons.

By Mr. GURNEY.—Did you not tell Mr. Thomas that you were determined to prosecute Church for having said disrespectful things of your wife?—I may have told him amongst other persons.

Did you not mention that, amongst other things, on that very morning that you had the interview with Mr. Church?—No; certainly not. Some other time I might.

By LORD ELLENBOROUGH.—Was it after that morning?—Yes, my Lord, it must have been a considerable time after that.

Re-examined by Mr. BOLLAND.

What did you inform him that you intended to institute a prosecution against Church for?—For defamation of my wife's character.

LORD ELLENBOROUGH.—That I suppose is your case?

Mr. MARRYATT.—No, my Lord, I am going to call Mrs. Hunter.

Mrs. HUNTER sworn.

Examined by Mr. MARRYATT.

I believe you are an attendant amongst the congregation, and a hearer of Mr. Church?—Yes.

Did he at any time write to you, early in the month of October last?—I received a letter in the beginning of the month of October, but there was no name to it.

There was no place of abode given, or any thing except the day of the month?—No.

Did you know from whom it came?—I cannot tell.

Did you put that letter into the hands of Mr. Patrick?—I gave it to Mr. Patrick's daughter, who gave it to her father.

Was that letter returned to you again?—It was; but I took no farther notice of it.

Was that letter returned to you again?—Yes.

You had a subpœna *duces tecum* to produce it?—I had but it is impossible to produce it.

Why is it impossible to produce it?—I will tell you why. After the letter was returned to me, I took no further notice of it. I put it into a drawer; but I know no more than his Lordship what is become of it; I looked for it on the Thursday morning before I came, but I could find no scraps of it. I was not able to find it.

Then you were wholly unable to find it?—I was.

By Lord ELLENBOROUGH.—Did you search diligently to find it?—I did, indeed, my Lord.

By Mr. MARRYATT.—Are you convinced there was no name to it?—I am.

Are you acquainted with Mr. Church's hand writing?—I have seen his writing, and I have seen it written in a different hand: not always alike, but sometimes very different: not to say exactly two different hands, but such a difference in the same hand writing, that you would hardly think it was the same. I have seen it so different, at times, that I should not at all times think it was the same.

Upon receiving the letter in question, whose hand writing did you believe it to be, and state it to be?

Mr. GURNEY.—I submit to your Lordship, that this is not a legal question.

Lord ELLENBOROUGH.—It is not evidence of the fact: but it is a proper question to refresh her recollection, as to whether she did not receive a letter which she believed to be the hand writing of the defendant.

By Mr. MARRYATT.—Whose hand writing did you think that letter to be?—I rather think it was Mr. Church's, but I could not be positive, as there was no name to it.

Do you now believe that letter to be Mr. Church's writing.—I cannot say whether it was or was not. It is not in my power.

By Lord ELLENBOROUGH.—You are not asked whether it was or was not: but what your belief was then, and what it is now?—I believed at that time, I must own, that it was his hand writing, and I still believe the same.

By Mr. MARRYATT.—Did you not then believe it to be Mr. Church's hand writing?—I did rather think it was.

Did you, or not, believe it was?—Is there any difference between *thinking* and *believing*?

That is a phrase we sometimes use in courts of justice.

I could not be positive; but I rather think it was his hand writing.

When you opened it, did you read it as a letter coming from him?—I was very much struck with the similarity, for it had very much the appearance of his hand writing; but, as no name was subscribed at the bottom, I could not be certain. It had the appearance of his hand writing.

Is it your belief now, that it was or was not, his hand writing?—It is exactly the same as it was then.

And it is now your belief that it was his hand writing?—I cannot say I firmly believe it, because it was not signed.

You are only asked whether you so acted as if it was his hand writing?—I did not communicate it to anybody but Mr. Patrick.

Did you communicate to Mr. Patrick that you had received a letter from Mr. Church?—I did.

Cross-examined by the COMMON SERJEANT.

The search which you made for this letter was not until last Thursday?—Exactly so.

For any thing you know, might it not be in your house now?—I have no reason to believe that it is, for I did not leave a drawer or place unsearched.

Lord ELLENBOROUGH.—As far as evidence can go of the loss of an original letter, to let in the copy, we have it in this case; for I asked her whether she made diligent search after the original, and she says, she has made diligent search.

Mr. Patrick *examined again by* Mr. MARRYATT.

Were you acquainted in October last with the hand-writing of Mr. Church?—Yes.

You told us you made this copy from the letter you had from Mrs. Hunter. Was the letter from which you made this copy, and which you returned to Mrs. Hunter, in your belief, the hand-writing of Mr. Church?—It was.

Mr. MARRYATT.—Now, my Lord, I propose reading this copy of the letter in question.

The following letter was then read in evidence:—

"*October* 6, 1816.

"DEAR MRS. HUNTER,

"My heart is already too much affected. Your letter only adds affliction to my bonds. But I forbear. I would have called on you this morning, but I was too low in mind to speak to any friend but Jesus! *There* I am truly comfortable. Pardon me; but I make no remarks on what you have been told. I must bear it, though I am able to contradict *three things* I would rather not. Mr. and Mrs. Patrick have always dealt kindly to me. I am only grieved that dear Mrs. P. whom I really loved, that she should try to injure me in the estimation of those who are real friends to my dear children. The thought affects me. Why hurt my poor family? But I am too much depressed to enlarge. I shall never forget their kindness. God will reward them, as he has many who have dealt well to me. But he will resent cruelty in those who have and are still trying to degrade me. Mrs. P. will live to see it. Dear Mrs. Hunter, I am grieved at heart I cannot relieve your mind. I am truly sorry to lose you as a hearer, because your soul has been blest; and you know both the plague of the heart and the value of Jesus. May he be increasingly present to you in his person, love, and grace! Farewell, my dear kind friend! The Lord Jesus will reward you for your love to me, and your kindness to mine. God is not unrighteous to forget your work of faith and labour of love. With many tears I write this. May we meet in glory, when no enemy shall distress my mind, nor sin nor death shall part us more! I need not remind my dear friend that I am a *Child* of *Peculiar Providence*; and that *heart* of eternal love, and that *arm* of invincible power has protected me—has called me to himself; and for every act of straying, will correct me with *his own hand*, but will resent *every other hand*, sooner or later. This you will live to see.

"Adieu, dear friend, accept the starting tear,
"And the best wishes of a heart sincere.

"Your's, truly,

"Till we shall meet above."

Mr. MARRYATT.—My Lord, that is the case on the part of the prosecution.

DEFENCE.

Mr. GURNEY then addressed the Jury on the part of the defendant, as follows:—

May it please your Lordship—

Gentlemen of the Jury—Gentlemen, I must agree with my Learned Friend, in entreating you to bestow your most serious attention upon this case, and in requesting you to consider (which, indeed, my Learned Friend fairly confessed you ought to bear in mind), that as the charge is heavy the proof ought to be clear; and that you will take care that your indignation against the crime shall have no influence upon your judgment respecting the person accused. That is a duty, Gentlemen, which is one of the most important, for a Juryman to attend to in this species of case, but it in one of most difficult performance; for such is, and such I trust ever will be, the feeling of abhorrence which Englishmen entertain against this detestable crime, that it is extremely difficult indeed, when a person is accused of it, to consider the case which in laid before us, in that dispassionate and unprejudiced manner, which is essential to the administration of justice. We all wish that no such occurrences could exist; and if a wish could blot them out of existence, we should be almost tempted to form that wish: but, Gentlemen, when these cases do come before us, they claim our very serious attention; and more particularly on this account, that it is a charge which, whenever made upon an individual, depends almost always upon the testimony of one witness, and where there is but one witness to make the accusation,—I mean one witness to the fact charged, so that the person accused can have no witness in his defence;—that, however innocent a man may be who is accused of this crime, provided the party is in a situation in which he cannot shew that he was fifty miles off at the time, it is quite impossible for him to have a witness to negative the fact. It must stand or fall upon the testimony of the principal witness, whose testimony, however, I need not tell you, is to be watched most scrupulously, and to be compared with the evidence of other witnesses; and if found inconsistent with the testimony of other witnesses, it is hardly then to be carried to the extent of full credence and of conviction.

Now, Gentlemen, the story which this young man has told you, is, upon his statement, a very extraordinary one, of the attack made upon him. Were any attack made upon him by Mr. Church, it would indeed be most extraordinary under the circumstances which he has stated. He represents himself to have been previously acquainted with him—that he had been one of his hearers— and yet from the hour of that acquaintance commencing, to the moment of this supposed abominable attack, that Mr. Church had never, either by word or gesture, made any indecent overture to him of any kind, signifying his intention, or had done any thing whatever to ascertain if he, the prosecutor, was ready to gratify any brutal of unnatural passion he might form. Now, it is a very extraordinary thing, that it should be supposed, that a person should get out of his own bed, and go to the bed of another, and commence the attack with the indecencies described by the witness, without any preparation of any kind whatever, without having any reason to believe, that the object of his attack would accede to his base, and unnatural purposes, with the full knowledge, (one should think,) that he was encountering certain detection and punishment, by the resistance that every man would be likely to make, to such an abominable attack; and it is, to be sure, most extraordinary to observe in what manner this is done. The young man states that he did not see the face of the person—that he felt the arm, and found that it was a shirt sleeve; but he did not feel any part of the flesh, so as to make any distinction between male und female; but he concludes that it was the shirt of a man, because the arm was covered down to the wrist. And when my Learned Friend, Mr. Marryatt, supposed that females are not covered down below the elbow, I have only to say, that I certainly always thought that females in their night clothes were covered down to their wrists. I ever understood that was the case; and therefore a person awakened out of sleep, in the fright that such a circumstance was likely to produce, and finding the arm of the person making the attack covered down to the wrist, would not, I think, be very well able to say whether it was the sleeve of a shirt or that of a woman's bed-gown; and that is all the means of knowledge which the witness has, as far as regards feeling the person.

Now I go on to the next evidence of identity. The next is the voice of the person who, he tells us, said in a feigned female voice, "Don't you know me, Adam? I am your mistress." Now, recollect, Gentlemen, the voice, it is thought, is a female voice; and whether it be feigned or not, depends upon his judgment and capacity of forming an opinion at a moment when he was in the greatest alarm and agitation; because if it was a female voice, then the voice was not feigned, and it could not be Mr. Church who was in the room. Now, I don't mean to suggest (far be it from me) that it was Mrs.

Patrick; but it is rather extraordinary and somewhat remarkable, considering the industry and the acrimony with which this case has been got up against Mr. Church, that they should not have produced Mrs. Patrick as a witness, and that they should think it right to withhold from your observation the other maid servant, who slept with Adam Foreman's sister. I think it is rather remarkable, that considering the industry with which I know this case was got up, they have not thought fit to produce that other female before you as a witness in order to say, "I was not out of my bed room that night, and I did not go into the apprentices bed room." Now, I think, that considering that the Prosecutors must have been aware of the powerful effect of such evidence, it is most surprising that they did not call forward the other persons in the house that night as witnesses, for the purpose of shewing, by their testimony, that they remained in their beds during the whole of that night, and for the purpose of giving some colour of probability to this very extraordinary and incredible story. But, no, Gentlemen, they choose to leave the case to the testimony of a frightened young man, wakened out of his sound sleep, and who, without seeing the face of Mr. Church, ventures to swear that the feigned female voice which he heard was that of the Defendant. I think, Gentlemen, in a case in which every thing depends, not so much upon his veracity, but upon the accuracy of his judgment in the course of his observation upon circumstances, with respect to which he was very little likely to draw any very accurate conclusions, that that servant ought to have been produced here, the more especially when the young man from the Pottery, going afterwards through the house for the purpose of seeing who was there, did find the female servant's door ajar; a circumstance not observable with respect to any other room in the house.

Now, I come to the next observation of identity; and I do think it is a most extraordinary one. There is a lamp, it seems, in the footpath of the terrace, five or six yards from the door. My Learned Friend, Mr. Bolland, inquired what sort of a lamp it was—whether it was a parish lamp, or a gas light? And he found by the answer, that it was the worst kind of lamp in the Metropolis—a parish lamp. Well, then, there is a dull parish lamp, five or six yards from the door, which gives a light through a large window—No, through a fan-light! and the person, whoever it is, opens the door to go out, and, as the door is opened the Lad sees that the person has a shirt on. Now, I beg to ask you, as men of sense and of experience in the world, whether it was possible for him to see whether that garment was a shirt, a shift, or a bed-gown—was it possible? Recollect, the light is not in the room—there is some light in the passage. The back of the person is towards him; and he is to tell you that it is Mr. Church, although he only saw his back! But then the next observation after the shirt, is as to the height of the person. Why, Gentlemen, nothing magnifies more than fright: nothing! We, all of us, have often heard the descriptions of persons in great fright. They always magnify the objects they see. If a person is robbed, the thief is a *monstrous tall man*! Why, Gentlemen, fright does magnify every object; and, therefore, we must make allowances for the situation in which this young man was placed at the time. He is disturbed in his sleep—the thing happens in a moment—and he sits up in his bed in a great fright—and he tells you it is Mr. Church, because of the height of the person he saw. Now if you can say that a person in that station is capable of distinguishing between a tall and a short person, I think it is a great deal too much in a case of this sort. But what has the person on his head? My Lord Ellenborough asked the question, *whether it was a man's* or woman's night-cap? and he says, "I cannot tell whether it was a night-cap or a handkerchief." And upon being asked the colour, he says, "I cannot tell." And there does not seem to be light enough to distinguish whether it was white or coloured. From this circumstance, therefore, Gentlemen, you will judge what sort of light there was to distinguish objects.

Now, Gentlemen, we come to the confirmation of this extraordinary story, particularly by Mr. Patrick. It is quite clear that Mr. Patrick has conceived some great anger against Mr. Church, on account of supposed slander of the character of his wife. Mr. Patrick himself is quite satisfied that his wife is not guilty, any more than the maid servant. But Mr. Patrick is angry, because he says, that Mr. Church has slandered the character of his wife. Why then, Mr. Patrick goes to Mr. Church, and he has some conversation with him. He tells him that he has seen some letter, but he does not mention what letter—he has seen some letter in which he, Mr. Church, has said that he could deny *three points* in the boy's story: and he puts questions to him, and he states to you, that Mr. Church having distinctly denied the indecent attack upon the boy, yet that he nevertheless admitted that he was in the room. Now, Gentlemen, upon that subject I must necessarily give you some evidence, as well as upon another part of this case; for I understand that Mr. Patrick distinctly stated to Mr. Thomas, who accompanied him as far as the house of Mr. Church, and whom he joined directly after he came out, that Mr. Church was not at all implicated; for on that occasion Mr. Thomas said to him, "Well, is there any thing against Mr. Church?" Upon which Mr. Patrick answered "No: Mr. Church is not all implicated." Mr. Patrick has denied it. I am told that Mr. Thomas will positively state that to have occurred. I am told so. Then, Gentlemen, if Mr. Patrick be contradicted in that most material circumstance—if you discredit him upon that part of the case, how can you give him credit in that part upon which my leaded friend fastened, as the confirmation of the story of the boy—"that he admitted to Mr. Patrick, that he had been in the boy's room." But the contradiction will not end there, Gentlemen. You have already one very important contradiction in the case; for the boy went directly to the Pottery, and he made a communication to West; and I asked him distinctly, and more than once, whether he stated to Mr. West that the person who attacked him in the manner he had described, had his hand upon his private parts? and he said that he had distinctly told Mr. West, that Mr. Church had laid his hand on his private parts: but, when West came to be examined, he told us that the boy did tell him that Mr. Church had behaved in a very indecent manner to him: but that he never, before the search was made, nor in the course of the night, nor from first to last, said a word to him about that circumstance.

Now, Gentlemen, that is a very strong contradiction of the story told you to-day by this man; and if that induces you to disbelieve him, or to doubt respecting his evidence, it will be impossible for you to find the Defendant guilty of this charge.

Gentlemen, I asked the boy at first, whether, instead of going to search in request of Mr. Church, he and the potter, West, had not gone to search for thieves? and he answered me, "Yes." But afterwards, he gave us some explanation, and said, "that he did not search the house particularly for thieves, but made a search to find if any body was about." Now, Gentlemen, upon this subject I am also enabled to give you some evidence, because I understand that both the boy and West distinctly stated, when they were before the Magistrate, that they did go and search the house for thieves, and that they made no other search but for thieves. Now, if there was any search made for thieves—if there was any notion in the mind of this boy that thieves were in the house, it would be quite impossible that he could be correct in the story he has told you to-day. And whether he has not magnified the thing—whether something which he has supposed to have happened between sleeping and awake that never happened—whether he has not been giving you a connected account now of what he had a confused notion then—is for your consideration.

But there is another circumstance respecting the case which is very important. The transaction, if it ever did take place, took place in the night of the 25th of September. On the 9th of October, and not until the ninth of October, does Mr. Patrick go to Mr. Church. There is a lapse of a fortnight. The witness whom I shall call to you will state, that after coming out from Mr. Church's, Mr. Patrick expressed himself satisfied that Mr. Church was not implicated. Now let us try that by the conduct of Mr. Patrick and of this boy. This is the 9th of October, and until the 12th of November no charge before a Magistrate is made. I beg to ask you whether the conduct of Mr. Patrick, in forbearing to make any charge before a Magistrate until the 12th of November, is not the strongest evidence that what my witness will state to you is true? That he was then satisfied that Mr. Church was not implicated in this abominable, odious, and unnatural transaction. Gentlemen, such charges ought never to be slept upon. No, not for an hour. If there be such a charge as that, and if it be really true that such things have taken place, no man ought to rest on it for a single hour.—

The charge ought to be made directly. But, what excuse is urged for this delay? "Oh," says my learned friend, "At last the transaction reached the ears of the apprentice's father." Why, you wont suppose that the apprentice's father had just returned from an East-India Voyage, and that the transaction coming to his ears on the 11th of November, he brought forward the charge. Gentlemen, there is no pretence for such an excuse. The boy slept at his father's. He did not sleep at his master's. Did he return to his father's house? His father lived within a quarter of a mile of Mr. Patrick, and he was in daily intercourse with his father, and had abundant opportunities of conferring with him upon the subject; and yet, for six weeks, no steps whatever are taken to bring Mr. Church before a Magistrate. My learned friend then told you that the father was the person who made the charge: but he has not called the father. The only person who appears here as the prosecutor is Mr. Patrick, and not the father; and they have not ventured to call the father as a witness; and there is no pretence made for the delay of this charge, unless it was that at this interview with Mr. Church, the prosecutor, Mr. Patrick, was satisfied, as I am told he expressed himself to be to the person who accompanied him, and waited at the door till he came out, that there was no ground for implicating the Defendant in this charge: and, Gentlemen, I say that his sleeping on the charge for upwards of a month after that interview with Mr. Church, is the strongest evidence that at that time he was satisfied of his innocence, and that this charge is brought forward on account of some anger, or some supposed declaration respecting Mr. Patrick's wife, which would make him extremely angry. If you find, Gentlemen, that there were no other motives than this to induce a charge of this kind, I have no doubt you will immediately acquit the Defendant.

Gentlemen, I have no further observations to make. The charge is most odious. The crime is most odious; and if it can be more attrocious in one person than another, it is in a person who is a public teacher of religion. If such a person, in defiance of every law human and divine. In contravention of those Sacred Scriptures, which it is his duty to read and expound, and having read and expounded them he can be found so far to forget every law of human nature and every principle of virtue, by the commission of this crime, he must be the most monstrous and attrocious of the human race, and no punishment can be adequate to his offences. But the punishment which must await him, would be infinitely worse than standing in the Court below to receive sentence for the completion of this attrocious crime; because I think that compared with instant death for the consummation of the crime, the being doomed to live the object of scorn, of hatred, and abhorrence by every human being, must be a punishment infinitely worse. Gentlemen, that is not too great for such monsters: but before you find the Defendant to be such, be satisfied by the whole of the evidence of his guilt. Compare the evidence on one side and on the other; and if it raises a doubt in your mind, the Defendant is entitled to the benefit of that doubt, and you will find him not guilty.

Mr. John Thomas *was the first witness called for the Defendant, and being sworn, was examined by the* COMMON SERJEANT.

Is your name John Thomas?—Yes.

Where do you live?—In Prospect-place, West's-square, St. George's-fields.

In what way of business are you?—An appraiser and undertaker.

Have you known Mr. Church long?—Yes.

Were you one of his hearers?—Yes.

Were you acquainted with Mr. Patrick?—Not till the report was made respecting Mr. Church.

Did you know him as one of the congregation attending Mr. Church?—No, I cannot say I did.

Were you with Mr. Patrick on any day that he went to Mr. Church's house—I mean on the 9th of October?—Yes, a few days after the report.

Did you go into the house with him?—No, I did not.

You were at the door?—I staid outside.

Had you learnt from Mr. Patrick that he was going to Mr. Church's upon the subject of this business?—Yes.

By Lord ELLENBOROUGH.—Did he tell you that he had a letter, and was going to make inquiries of Mr. Church?—He called upon me at my house to go with him.

By the COMMON SERJEANT.—And told you he was going to Mr. Church's upon the business of this inquiry?—Yes; indeed it was my request that he should. Mr. Thomas went to speak to his wife; and it was at my wife's request and Mrs. Patrick's I believe that he went.

Your wife joined in her request?—Yes.

How long might his interview with Mr. Church last—how long was he in the house?—He seemed to be a long while; not much less than an hour.

As near as you could guess, the time, was it near an hour?—Yes.

When he came out did you put any questions to him respecting what had passed between; him and Mr. Church?—Yes.

What questions did you put?—I asked him what Mr. Church had said.

What answer did he give you?—He said that Mr. Church did not say any thing. He said Mr. Church seemed very much confounded on account of the cause, he supposed, but he said nothing about it; that it would be injurious to the cause of God. He did not say the *cause of God*, but I only supposed he meant the cause of God.

By Lord ELLENBOROUGH.—Did he use the words "cause of God?"—No, he said Mr. Church seemed very much confounded or confused.

Then the rest is all imagination of your's?—We both imagined alike. I don't know that these were exactly the words, for I cannot call to my mind what he did say; but it was conjectured the cause of God, and which we heard afterwards was abused abroad.

You are now called, Sir, for the purpose of contradiction. You are recollecting the effect, you know, of a conversation and communication with Mr. Patrick, and you must say truly what passed, if you can recollect it.—I don't recollect all that passed.

By the COMMON SERJEANT.—When you were stopt in your account of what passed, you were going to say something. You were asked whether Mr. Church had said any thing to Mr. Patrick which Mr. Patrick related to you. What did he say?—He said, No. He said Mr. Church seemed very much confused.

What did you ask Mr. Patrick next?—"Why," said I, "what do you mean. Why, if you know any thing against the man, did you not charge him with it? I would have been very faithful with him, and charged him with it."

What answer did Mr. Patrick make to that?—He said he did not know; he was not the person.

By Lord ELLENBOROUGH.—Repeat that in Mr. Patrick's own words. Attend, and wait to hear the question. Be so good as to suppose that you were narrating the conversation as it occurred with Mr. Patrick. Instead of saying, *He*, say *I*. Attend now.

By the COMMON SERJEANT.—What further did he say? and give his own words.—He said, "I don't know: I am not so proper a person as you," or words to the same effect. I said to him, "What did he (meaning Church) say respecting the report?"

What had the report reference to that you spoke of?—The report respecting this transaction.

What answer did Patrick make to that? What did Patrick say to you when you put the question, as to what Church had said respecting the report?—I said to Mr. Patrick, says I, "what did he say respecting the acknowledging the report"—that is, what did Mr. Church say to Mr. Patrick about acknowledging the report that had gone abroad respecting him. He said, "It was false."

Do you mean that Church said it was false?—I mean that Patrick said that the report was false.

By Lord ELLENBOROUGH.—That is not the answer to the question put by the Gentleman. Did Church say that it was false?—I never saw Church upon the subject.

By the COMMON SERJEANT.—When Patrick made you an answer, did you understand that answer to be, that Church had said the report was false, or that Patrick himself said the report was false?—Patrick himself.

Patrick himself said that the report was false?—Certainly.

Did you then put any other question to Mr. Patrick?—I did.

What other question did you put?—I said, what answer did Mr. Church give respecting its having been reported that he was in liquor—that he made an excuse that he was in liquor?

What answer did Mr. Patrick give to that?—He said it was false. He said there had been a great deal of exaggeration.

Did you after this put any question to Mr. Patrick, whether he, Mr. Patrick, thought that Mr. Church was implicated in the transaction or not? Did you put any such question to him?

Lord ELLENBOROUGH.—Did you use those words, or words to the same effect?—No, I did not I put these words to him—"Why," says I, "you did nothing! Did Mr. Church acknowledge nothing to you?" "No, Sir," says he, "he did not." Then he said Mr. Church had not mentioned a word about it.

Did you make any observation to him, or he to you?—I don't recollect any thing in particular. I said, says I, "As you can bring nothing against him, let us pray for him, and if he had the least idea of such a thing; and as you say you cannot bring any thing home to him, and can't prove any thing, that is all we can do. Let us pray that he may not be guilty of such sin."

Lord ELLENBOROUGH.—Did you say, pray for him, if he was under any such temptation?—Yes; pray for him, if was under any such temptation.

THE COMMON SERJEANT.—Did Mr. Patrick after that deliver any opinion to you whether he thought Church was implicated in the transaction or not?—No, he did not.

Did you at any other time see him, and hear him say any thing about this transaction?—No.

Did any thing more pass at this meeting than what you have told us? No.—Yes, Sir. I ask pardon: I met him in June last, coming over Waterloo-bridge. I did not at first know him; and he spoke to me, and he said, "My name is Patrick." I said, "Mr. Patrick, why what are you doing with Mr. Church?" "Why," says I, "I hear you have brought something else against him: what is that?"

Lord ELLENBOROUGH.—There is no contradiction of Mr. Patrick in this. He was not asked to this (continuation of the answer). "Why," says he, "Sir, I should not have done it, but that Mr. Church has spoken more disrespectful things respecting Mrs. Patrick." He said he should not have done it, but that Mr. Church had said many disrespectful things of Mrs. Patrick.

Cross-examined by Mr. MARRYATT.

Was it the Sabbath after the 27th of September that you first heard of this?—I believe it was. It was within two or three days after.

I think we have learnt that upon the Thursday night Mr. Patrick came home, and that on the Friday morning the boy communicated to him what had happened. Now on the Saturday, was not this matter currently talked of about Mr. Church?—No, I believe not.

You mean that you heard of the report two or three days after the thing happened?—Yes.

You then heard of the report?—Yes.

You told us that you were desirous that Mr. Patrick should call on Mr. Church?—Yes.

Then he did so, at your desire?—Yes.

Did Mr. Patrick bring the boy to you, and offer to have him brought face to face with Mr. Church?—I believe he did.

Mr. Patrick said the boy was outside?—Mr. Patrick called at my house in the course of the morning, and he sent him, and he said the boy was outside.

Did he wish you to see the boy?—Not particularly, I believe.

For what purpose did he bring the boy?—To go to Mr. Church's?—I supposed so.

To go with you or with him, or with both of you to Mr. Church's?—I was to go with him, and therefore the boy followed.

Did the boy go with him into Mr. Church's house?—He staid outside the door. He walked on the other side of the way, opposite to where I was.

But he waited whilst you waited?—Yes: we both waited outside.

Ready to go in to Mr. Church's when you were wanted?—Yes: Mr. Patrick was to go in and hear what Mr. Church had to say; and then we were to go in, too.

And he took the boy with him, in order that he might be taken in and see Mr. Church face to face?—He brought the boy with him, and I suppose that was his intention.

Did you decline introducing the boy to Mr. Church?—I had no particular acquaintance with Mr. Church?—I was only one of his hearers, and I thought it would be too great a liberty for me to go to him. Mr. Patrick wanted me to go in alone to Mr. Church, first.

Did he not invite you to take the boy in with you?—He said nothing about that; I don't recollect any thing that he did.

Why did you tell me, then, that you supposed the purpose of bringing the boy was that he should be introduced to Mr. Church?—No doubt about that. I don't know any other reason he had than that, for bringing the boy.

Did he say so?—I don't know that he said that that was his reason. He said he had the boy there.

Do you remember your declining to go in with Mr. Patrick to Mr. Church's?—I told him I had no particular interest in the business. I had no intimacy with Mr. Church, except hearing him. I thought I had no business to be interested in the knowledge of the fact, being only a hearer. I thought therefore that my visit would be obtrusive.

Because you had no particular interest in the business?—Why, I certainly had no interest in it.

And therefore you declined going in and taking the boy with you?—I saw no necessity of so doing, as he did not acknowledge himself guilty of any thing bad.

By Lord ELLENBOROUGH. But the boy being there, had you not the curiosity to examine the boy?—I did not, it being delicate subject.

Did you not think it important to come at the truth upon the subject, as the boy was there and you might have examined him yourself?—If Mr. Church had confessed any thing, I should have thought it my duty to take the boy and have them face to face.

But I should have thought that the circumstance of his not confessing would be the reason why you would take them face to face; or else why should you take the boy at all. But Mr. Church not having confessed any thing, you therefore would not examine the boy.—Was that your reason for not examining the boy?—Yes, my Lord.

By Mr. BOLLAND.—But if he confessed any thing, you would have taken the boy to have them face to face?—Yes.

Your object was to take the boy and have them face to face, if Mr. Church acknowledged the crime?—Yes.

But surely when you found that Mr. Church had acknowledged his fault, then there would be no reason for taking the boy to have them face to face?—I should have thought it proper to take the boy in, if Mr. Church acknowledged his crime. I wished the boy in fact to come in with us; but when Mr. Patrick came out and said that Mr. Church did not acknowledge any thing of it, I did not think it necessary to have them face to face.

Then you did not think it right to have the boy in?—I never spoke to the boy.

You never asked the boy about this transaction?—No.

Mr. Patrick never gave any opinion whether Mr. Church was implicated in the transaction; but in answer to a particular part of the transaction, he said that Mr. Church asserted that it was false?—Yes.

Did you see the letter sent to Mrs. Hunter?—No.

I mean the letter about the three points of the boy's statement which Mr. Church said he was able to contradict?—No.

Mr. JAMES REEVES *sworn.*

Examined by the COMMON SERJEANT.

Were you the Clerk attending the Magistrate when the charge was made before him;—I was.

Who was the Magistrate?—I must refer to the book—(*Witness produced a book.*)

That is your minute book in which you enter the proceedings of the day?—Yes.

Who was the sitting Magistrate on that day?—Mr. Serjeant Sellon appears to have been the Magistrate on the 19th of November, as it appears by the book.

This being a charge of misdemeanor, do you find by your book that any account was committed to writing of what the witnesses said?—No; it was not. It is merely a note, or entry of the names, as follows: "Warrant for a misdemeanor, parties appeared by the Officer, and ordered to find bail."

Cross-examined by Mr. MARRYATT.

Was that the Magistrate by whom the warrant was granted?—Yes.

Was the oath administered before the warrant was granted?—Yes; there had been an *ex-parte* examination to grant the warrant on the oath of the party.

That is in another book?—It is; that is left behind; I do not know any thing of it.

But there is a deposition on oath prior to the granting of the warrant?—Yes.

Re-examined by the COMMON SERJEANT.

The depositions in cases of misdemeanour you don't take in detail?—No.

Were the depositions taken in writing in any book which you have not here?—I am not aware of that.

Lord ELLENBOROUGH.—You were not told to bring it?—No.

Was that the only information upon which the warrant was granted?—There was nothing taken down in writing when all the parties were before the Magistrate.

Were the depositions taken down before the warrant was granted?—Yes.

Then, after the warrant was executed, and at the time of the examination when the Defendant was there, you took no minutes?—No farther than the names of the parties; and what I have here.

Mr. WOOD *sworn*.

Examined by Mr. Gurney.

Were you present at the examination of Mr. Church before the Magistrate?—I was.

What are you?—A hatter, near the Elephant and Castle, in St. George's Fields.

Lord ELLENBOROUGH.—Did you take the testimony of the witnesses down in writing?—No.

Mr. GURNEY.—Did Foreman, the boy, in the account he gave before the Magistrate, say for what purpose he searched the house?—He said that he went out to the Potter and told the Potter that there were thieves in the house, and that the Potter and he came to search the house. He was asked a question by Mr. Sellon, whether or no he searched the room where Mr. Church slept. He said, No, he did not search that room. Mr. Sellon said, "Why not search that room?"

What answer did he give to that?—The answer he gave was that the Potter wished to break the door open. Mr. Sellon said, "Did you try the door to see whether it was open, before the Potter talked of breaking it open?" He said, No: he did not wish to disturb his mistress.

Whilst the Potter was examined, did he say what was the alarm that Foreman gave to him; did he say what was the alarm?—I cannot charge my memory as to that.

Mr. GURNEY.—My Lord, this is the case of the Defendant.

Mr. MARRYATT then replied to the Defendant's case, as follows:—

May it please your Lordship, Gentlemen of the Jury—My learned Friend has almost admitted the case on the part of the Prosecution, in the nature of his address to you, by saying, in effect, that if you believed Mr. Church to have gone into the boy's chamber at that unseasonable hour of the morning, he could hardly come there for any purpose but that ascribed to him by this Indictment. At least, if my Learned Friend did not make that confession in terms so explicitly as I have given them, certainly he has not offered in his address to you the smallest explanation of so very suspicious a purpose. And although I invited him, when I first had the opportunity of stating this case, to assign any possible reason, except that which is imputed to the Defendant as matter of crime, why he should be in the Boy's room under such circumstances, we have had no motive assigned, nor any suggestion of apology or excuse offered for such conduct.

There is an improbability in this case it is contended; because there had been no overture of the same description made to the lad before this period, nor any circumstance, by which an indication of the Defendant's unnatural propensities, prior to this transaction, could be inferred. Gentlemen, we have lived some time in the world, and we have seen that men, with these diabolical passions, make those overtures, not unfrequently, to persons they never saw in the whole course of their lives, until some occasional meeting—sometimes in the Parks—nay, sometimes, even at public assemblies; and yet so extraordinary is the phrenzy with which men of these propensities are hurried, there is no accounting for their conduct on these occasions: certainly there is no amounting for the conduct of this Defendant in going into the boy's chamber, except that which his abominable and unnatural lusts can suggest, and which are imputed to him by this indictment. Gentlemen, in the first place, was he there? Why it is suggested that the boy's fright had magnified the powers of his vision, and that he must have mistaken the Defendant for his mistress, or for the maid servant, who slept with his sister. Now, Gentlemen, we have it in evidence that Mr. Church is a man near six feet high: a man of considerable size, and distinguishable from the boy's mistress, who is a little feminate figure; and also very distinguishable from the maid servant, whom my learned friend, Mr. Gurney, wishes you to infer was the person who entered the prosecutor's room, because the maid's chamber door was not shut; although there was no question asked by the Defendant's Counsel, as to the intimacy of this young man with that servant maid. I admit that the servant's door was not fast; but my Learned Friend did not inquire whether the servant's door had been left open or fastened, when the servants went to bed; nor was any inquiry made whether the lock of that door was defective, as sometimes happens to be the case with the servant's rooms in a gentleman's house; for deficiencies of that description are not so immediately remedied as in the more preferable rooms of the house. Gentlemen, could the young man by any possibility mistake the female figure of the maid servants or of his mistress, for the man he described—a man that is of considerable size—near six feet high, and a very striking object in point of height? Most unquestionably there is no pretence for supposing, that there could be any body else but Mr. Church in the room at that time. Now what is the conduct of the young lad on that occasion? He goes down to West, the potter, immediately, and states to him, that Mr. Church had behaved indecently. I admit that, in the course of conversation, he mentioned some of the particulars of what occurred, which the potter says he does not recollect. The boy goes on further, and states particulars that he had related to the man, which the latter says had not been mentioned to him; and what is more probable, than that in giving an account of a conversation which took place so long ago as the month of September last, that the one may add half a sentence which the other does not remember? But was not the statement that the lad made at the time to the second witness, West, (though the latter does not recollect the whole of what passed) that Church came into his chamber, and conducted himself with indecency towards him? They then return to the house; the lad and he examine the house for the purpose of ascertaining whether any body else is there; no other male person sleeping in the house; and they find all secure and safe; and yet it is to supposed, that they went in search for thieves! Why the result of the search would decide whether the object of the search was to see whether there were any thieves in the house—for neither a door nor a window had been opened, nor was there any aperture at which a thief could gain admittance. It is clear, therefore, that there was no other male in the house except Church, the party indicted; nor is there now any colour for supposing that there was any body else there of his sex but himself. But, it is said their object was to search for thieves, and that the alarm was for thieves, and that the Boy, when he went before the Magistrate, gave some account about searching for thieves. Why, in his examination here to-day, when he was asked whether he and West did not go back together to the house and search for thieves, he very naturally said, "Yes, Sir:" but why did he give that answer?—Because there was another proposition put to him, which appeared as material as that with respect to the search for thieves, and accordingly he answered in the affirmative. It is true that he did admit at first, that he went to search for thieves; but when he came to give the explanation to the answer, he states that he did not particularly search for thieves; and after a little cross-examination by the same Learned Counsel, it appeared that the object was not to search for thieves, but merely to ascertain that there was no other man in the house that could possibly commit this indecency, this outrage against religion, morality, and nature. But the man who was called last, named Wood, is called to state something that passed before the Magistrate; and, according to his representation, there was something said about going to search for thieves. It is observable, however, that he did not take up the whole story told in the testimony of the lad, nor did my Learned Friend examine him as to the anterior part of his statement: and from this it must fairly be inferred, that the most material part of the boy's testimony given to-day, and that given before the Magistrate, was consistent, and not to be shaken. For you may be quite certain, Gentlemen, that when my Learned Friends on the other side content themselves with catching at the smallest variance in the testimony of the witness from his original statement; it is a decided proof that the most important part of the case is not to be shaken, and is incapable of contradiction. The material part of the evidence remains untouched by any shadow of doubt as to its credibility. My Learned Friend rests satisfied with the contradiction upon the subject of what passed between the Potter and the Boy, but which, I say, is wholly immaterial as it affects his credit; and the only further objection he makes to his testimony is, that his evidence of to-day does not correspond, in some minute particular, with his examination before the Magistrate. For the reasons, however, which I have given you, Gentlemen, you will dismiss these trifling matters from your serious consideration.

But it seems that Mr. Patrick has been guilty of some mis-statement as to what occurred in the early stage of this proceeding; and we have Mr. Thomas called, as it is said, for the purpose of contradicting him, as to the result of some conversation which passed between them after the interview at Mr. Church's house. Gentlemen, it is some what singular that Mr. Thomas, who was one of the Defendant's hearers, and interested himself so much in this case, that when the boy is brought to give him information as to the complaint which he had to make against Mr. Church, he does not make the least inquiry into the lad's account of the transaction, nor does he express any desire that the lad should be introduced to Mr. Church. We have it in evidence from himself, that on the day when Mr. Patrick called upon Mr. Church, he waited with the lad on the outside of the house; and although Mr. Patrick brought the boy for the express purpose of having him confronted face to face with the Defendant, still Mr. Thomas does not ask a single question of the lad, nor does he go into any examination upon the subject.

Gentlemen, that this case was immediately blazoned about very early is clear, though it was not carried before the magistrate so soon; because we find that when Mr. Patrick came home on the Thursday night, though he did not speak to the boy until the next day, the Friday, yet the subject was generally mentioned to his wife before he returned, and therefore the matter might have got wind before it was fully explained by the boy to his master on the Friday morning. It is quite clear that it was known to the congregation on the following sabbath, and according to that letter which has been read to you, (upon which I make no comments, except so far as it bears on Mr. Patrick's testimony), the Defendant, Mr. Church, had written on the 6th of October to Mrs. Hunter, Mrs. Hunter having previously written to him on the subject, for he begins by referring to the letter which Mrs. Hunter had addressed to and expresses regret that he shall lose her as a hearer in future: so that Mrs. Hunter therefore, amongst other persons, was acquainted with the rumours, because from him this letter comes, from which it appears that she had written to him before; for it begins by stating—"My heart is already too much affected: your letter only added affliction to my bonds."— Gentlemen, I only dwell upon this circumstance in confirmation of Mr. Patrick's statement, that Mr. Church could contradict, not the whole of the report, but three points of the boy's statement. This letter having come to the knowledge of Mr. Patrick, in which these three points are alluded to, and being desired by some of the congregation to pay the Defendant a visit, he accordingly resolves to call upon him. On that occasion he introduces himself by stating, as the apology for his calling, that he had seen a letter from the Defendant, in which he stated that he could contradict certain points of the boy's story. The Defendant you will observe does not contradict the fact of his having written such a letter, but he goes into an explanation with the witness as to what are the points of contradiction; and then he states that so far as his having laid hold of the boy, and his having told the lad that the person who addressed him was his mistress, the whole was a mis-statement; and these, Gentlemen, are the only points of denial upon which the Defendant rested in his interview with Mr. Patrick, to whom, however, he admitted distinctly that he was in the boy's chamber, though he denies the subsequent part of the transaction, which the boy to-day has solemnly sworn to have taken place.

Now, gentlemen, I ask again, if he was in the boy's chamber, for what reason or proper purpose could he by possibility go there? And if he was in that room, can you have any doubt of the truth of all the circumstances which the boy has positively sworn?—If it was a person of the male sex who entered that apartment, it must clearly have been the defendant; for there was no other man in the house. It appearing distinctly that Mr. Patrick was absent from home on that night. Then I ask you, whether there is any ground for disbelieving the boy's story, who, immediately after the disgusting scene he has described, goes to the pottery, tells his story to the workman, and stays there the remainder of the night, chusing rather to lose his rest than stay in the house with Mr. Church, under the liability of a further encounter for the same detestable purpose. The reason which the boy has given for not alarming the house, is not an unnatural one. We have it in evidence that Mr. West, feeling a manly indignation at what had happened, manifested a disposition to pull the unnatural offender out of his bed, and turn him into the street. But the boy, apprehensive that such an occurrence might give an alarm to his mistress, persuaded the potter to abstain from his purpose, and they accordingly did not enter the defendant's door.

Thus, gentlemen, the testimony of the prosecutor is consistent in all its parts; for although Church denied some circumstances of the transaction as stated in his letter read to-day, yet every main and important feature of the transaction is confirmed by collateral circumstances. Mr. Patrick's evidence is a direct corroboration of the boy's story, from the moment that the transaction first took place down to his examination of to-day. But if, gentlemen, as I said before, you feel any reasonable doubt of the purpose for which the defendant came into the boy's room, it is your duty to acquit him; but, on the other hand, if all the circumstances of the case conspire to imprint upon your mind that the defendant had clearly no other purpose, but a guilty and unnatural one when he entered that apartment, it is your bounden duty, disgusting as it may be, to pronounce a sentence of condemnation, whatever consequences may result to the defendant in the judgment which he shall hereafter receive.

THE CHARGE.

Lord Ellenborough delivered his charge to the jury as follows:

Gentlemen of the Jury—This is an indictment against John Church for an assault upon the person of Adam Foreman, with intent to commit an unnatural crime with him. There has been a considerable body of evidence laid before you, against him as well as for him: and it is for you to say in the result, after giving that evidence due consideration, whether the defendant has committed the assault with intent to perpetrate the atrocious crime imputed to him by the indictment.

Now, assuming the fact to be that Mr. Church was in the room at the time this offence was supposed to have been committed, that alone imposes upon him the necessity of giving some explanation for the occasion which brought him there. If, in addition to the fact of being there, which he admits, himself, to be true, you should believe the boy further in his statement that such an overture was made to him, and that the hand of a man was put upon his private parts in bed, you will have to say with what other purpose than as an inducement to the commission of an unnatural crime, it had been placed there. That is, supposing you believe the facts as stated by the young man. I should apprehend that no reason can be suggested for such an indecent intercourse (supposing it did take place) with this man's person unless it was a prelude or inducement to the committing of the crime imputed to the defendant. Now the main question for your consideration will be, whether that which is sworn by Foreman, and confirmed by Mr. Patrick, is truly sworn. I think too much stress has been laid upon the circumstance, stated about the searching for thieves, which it is said, on the part of the defendant, was the avowed object of Foreman in returning to the house. It was very natural and highly probable when he apprehended, if he did truly apprehend, that a male person had come into his room and had accosted him in the manner he stated, that he should be clearly satisfied before he went farther in communicating to the potter the indecencies offered to his person, that there was no other male in the house, and seeing that no other male could come into the house at that time of night, unless he came for this purpose and no other. In this point of view, I think it is not at all unnatural or improbable in his conduct, even if he had said that he had gone in search for thieves; and, if you recollect, his evidence was, "that he had searched the house, not for thieves in particular, but to see if there was any body in any of the rooms." "I did not think of thieves," says he, "because I knew who it was," and so on. He now says, that at that time he knew it was Mr. Church, and therefore he did not think of searching for thieves, his object being, in searching the house, to ascertain whether there was any other male in the house besides the one to whom he attaches the crime imputed by this indictment.

Gentleman, I shall now proceed to state to you the evidence as it has been given on both sides.

Adam Foreman, the first witness, states, that he shall be twenty years of age the first day of December next. "I am an apprentice to, Mr. Patrick, the potter, of Vauxhall; I have been with him about five years. I have known the defendant, John Church, by sight about two or three years. He is a preacher, and I have attended as one of the congregation in the chapel where he preaches; I have often seen him. I sleep generally at my father's house, but when my master goes out of town I sleep at his house. The defendant Church lives near his chapel in St. George's Fields. The defendant came to sleep at my master's on the 25th of September last." It seems, Gentlemen, he came there by invitation from Mr. Patrick, having weak health, and it being more convenient for him to sleep in better air. "He slept there on the night of the 25th September; I slept there also, that night. I don't know whether the defendant had been there before; I cannot say whether I had seen him there before. My master was out of town that night, but where I cannot say. The persons who slept in the house that night were Mr. Church, my mistress, the children, and the two maid-servants; there was no other man in the house except Church and myself. My bed-room was the front parlour on the first floor, over the kitchen. It was not usually a bed-room, but I slept there because there was no other bed-room that I could sleep in. A temporary bed was put up there for me. I went to bed at near one o'clock. There was a kiln burning, and I was obliged to sit up to let the man in to the kiln when he came. It was necessary for me to sit up to attend that kiln, and to give the man the key. That man's name is Thomas West. I went to sleep directly I went to bed. I had not been asleep more than half an hour, before I was awoke by some one putting his hands under the bed clothes, and laying hold of my private parts. He laid hold of me very tight. I put my hand out of the bed clothes and caught hold of him, and asked him who he was. I said, who are you? I laid hold of him, as near as I can guess, by the upper part of the arm; and I felt lower down, and found by the sleeve that he had got a man's shirt on. I had a hold of him by the upper part of the arm, and running my hand down to the wrist, I found he had a man's shirt on. The wrist was buttoned. I knew very well it was man, because he had got a man's shirt on. The person, whoever it was, said, in a feint voice like a woman, "Adam, don't you know me? I am your mistress." It was not Mrs. Patrick's voice. I knew the voice directly I heard it to be Mr. Church's. He fled from the room directly; he went out of the room in a hurried step. I got out of bed and put on my small clothes and shoes, and went out to the door. As the man opened the door, I saw by the lamp that it was Mr. Church, and he had only his shirt on. The lamp is outside of the street door, on the Terrace, and throws a light through the fan-light of the hall door. It is a parish lamp. At the time I saw Church by the light of the lamp I was sitting up in bed: I had not then left my bed. I saw that the person who went out through the door had a man's shirt on. I did not see his face at all; his back was to me. I then got up and put my small-clothes on and shoes, and went to the pottery to get the man to come up to the house. I told Thomas West what had happened. He was in the pottery, and was there I before went to bed. The person who went out at the door shut it after him. I saw him by the light of the lamp when he opened the door. There was no light in the room; the light came from a lamp on the terrace. That lamp is about five or six yards from the door of the house on the terrace. The terrace, on which my master's house is situated, is a row of houses raised above the road. The lamp is upon the terrace opposite to the door. The light from the lamp is given to the passage through the fan-light over the door. When the man opened the door and went out, I saw him by the light from the lamp. I could not see the face of the person, but I saw that he had a shirt on. I was rather alarmed. It all took place in a minute. It was not long about. I don't know how long he had been there before I awoke. From the moment I awoke it took place as fast as possible. I immediately went to West. We did not know whether any body had got in or not. West and I directly came and searched the house for thieves. We went and looked at every chamber door in the home except Mr. Church's and my mistress's. We looked at the door of Mr. Church, and that of my mistress. They were both shut. We found all the doors in the house shut except the servant's, which we found on the jar."

Now, Gentlemen, great stress is laid by the learned counsel for the Defendant upon this circumstance. It is suggested that it might be Mrs. Patrick, or one of the maid servants who entered the room. It appears that one of the servants was the prosecutor's own sister, and it was not likely to be her that went in. It is said the prosecutor's counsel ought to have called the maid servant and Mrs. Patrick to negative the supposed circumstance of their having gone into the room. Now, this observation is to be made, that it was open to the one side or to the other to have called the maid servant, and have proposed that question to her. It was clearly open to the Defendant, if he chose to call the maid, and to have asked her that question; and it was equally open to the counsel for the prosecution. It was also open to both sides to have called Mrs. Patrick. It is probable that the prosecutor's counsel did not like to expose her to the pain of an unnecessary examination, because the Defendant might have called her as a witness for himself.

"I went and told West that Mr. Church came down into my room, and behaved in a very indecent manner. I told him that Church had been there and laid hold of my private parts. I did not search the house for thieves in particular, but to search if any body was in any of the rooms. We searched the house. We looked all over it to see if there was anybody in any of the rooms. We searched the house, but not for thieves in particular. I did not think of thieves, because I knew who it was. We did not go into the maid servant's room; we only looked in. We found the door open and looked in. The maids were in bed. One was my sister. The door being a-jar, we pushed a little, and we saw that they were a-bed. We did not speak to them. We did not search the house for thieves, because I knew who the person was. The reason of my searching the house was because I wished to be quite right before I made the accusation against Mr. Church. We found that there was no other man in the house but Mr. Church. There was no door, no window open, at which any other man could have come in. The light from the Terrace came through the fan-light over the door. The lamp gives a pretty fair light to the hall, and shews a little light up the stairs. The time when the person opened the door and went out, was the time that I got a view of his person. I did not hear him when he first came into the room. I was awakened by the application of his hand to my person. He was standing by the bed-side on the floor. I did not call to him by name, or give him to understand that I knew who he was. I did not see any part of his face, but I saw his back as he went out of the room. He was a person that appeared to be the height of Mr. Church. I cannot say what height he is. I cannot say exactly whether he had a night-cap on. I think it was a handkerchief tied round his head. I could not tell what sort of a handkerchief it was, whether coloured or not."

He does not say positively whether it was a light or a coloured handkerchief, but he says he could not tell. He did not see whether it was coloured or not.

"We went to Church's door, but we did not touch it, nor did we go in. West wanted to go into the room and pull him out."

That is confirmed by the testimony of West himself.

"I objected to West's pulling him out, because I was afraid of disturbing my mistress. She would have been very much alarmed."

That was the account he gave in his original examination before the magistrate, as the reason for his not going into the room.

"Church never had any conversation with me, nor did he ever make any overture of this sort to me before this time. There was nothing particular in his manner or in his conduct towards me before this time. I have never spoken to him at all since. I saw him attend before the magistrate. There I spoke in his presence, but not immediately to him. I did not hear him speak before the magistrate. I have given the same account before the magistrate that I have now done here. I know no other circumstances from which I could collect that it was a man. The hand was withdrawn when I awoke. By the height of the person I saw, I could ascertain whether it was or was not the height of my mistress or any of the female part of the house. Mr. Church was a great deal bigger than any body there. I don't think he is quite six foot. He is a tall and stout man. There was light enough by the lamp to see the outline of the man, so as to be able to say that he was a tall person. Mrs. Patrick is quite a little woman, she is quite different person from the person I saw in the room. I am quite clear of that. The maid who slept in the room with my sister, is about as tall as I am; not quite so tall. I am quite sure it was not her. There was no other maid in the house."

This is the evidence of the first witness; and you observe he says, he is quite sure it was not any of the females of the house who came into his room; and he is quite sure that there was no other male person in the house besides himself and the Defendant Church; and he is certain that it was not the maid nor his mistress.

The next witness examined is Thomas West. He says, "I am workmen to Mr. Patrick, the potter. On the morning of the 26th of September last, I relieved Adam Foreman at the Kiln. I relieved him about half past twelve o'clock in the morning: he left me shortly afterwards for the purpose of going to bed. I saw him again in about half an hour. He was only part dressed. He had his small clothes, his shoes, and one stocking on. He came to me in a very great fright, and bid me light my candle. He appeared very much alarmed, and bid me light my candle and come along with him up to the house. He told me, as we were going along the garden, that Mr. Church had been to him, and behaved in a very indecent manner. He did not explain how. He unlocked the door, and we went into the house together. When we got into the house he put the remainder of his clothes on. We then went and searched every room in the house, beginning at the bottom and going upwards to the top, except my mistress's room and Mr. Church's. We went into all the rooms except Mr. Church's and Mrs. Patrick's. We did not go into Mr. Church's room or that of my mistress. We did not open the door of either of those two rooms. When we came to Mr. Church's door, I said, "I'll go and pull him out; shall I?" The Lad said, "No, for fear of disturbing my mistress." In consequence of that observation of the lad's, I forebore going into the room. Foreman then came along with me into the Pottery. He came down stairs; locked the back door, and staid with me the whole of the remainder of the night at the Pottery 'till the morning. We searched in all the rooms of the house for the purpose of seeing if there was any other person in the place. We found no window or door open at which any body could have got into the house. I saw them all secure and fastened. When Foreman came to me, he did not explain what Church had done to him; he only told me that Church had behaved in a very indecent manner to him. I did go to search for thieves in the house. When he told me that Church had behaved in a very indecent manner to him, I went to see if there was any other person in the place. Foreman did not tell me he believed that there was thieves in the house. I am quite sure he did not explain in what way Church behaved to him. He did not tell me that Church came to his bed side, and laid his hand upon his private parts; he never from first to the last, either in the course of the morning when staying with me, or after we had been to the house, tell me what Church had done, and that he had laid his hand upon his private parts. I went before the Magistrate some time after this; I believe it was six or seven weeks."

Gentlemen, there would be a great deal in the observation upon the circumstance of the parties not going before the Magistrate until six or seven weeks afterwards, if the matter had been kept a secret. But it is not kept a secret; so far from that, it was quite notorious. And here is a letter, in the hand-writing of the Defendant himself, dated the 6th of October, in answer to a letter of Mrs. Hunter; and it appears that the subject had been ventilated and circulated, for some days before, and had become the topic of general discussion amongst the Defendant's congregation; because it appears that Mrs. Hunter had written a letter herself to the Defendant upon it. There is nothing, therefore, in the observation of the Learned Counsel for the Defendant as to the tardiness of going before the Magistrate.

He says, "The Lad then went with his father. The Lad generally slept at home at his father's house. The father lives about a quarter of a mile from Mr. Patrick's. The Boy did not sleep at his father's the next night; but he did the next night after that. We did not go to the Justices until about six or seven weeks afterwards. I did not communicate with Mr. Patrick upon the subject before I went to the Justice."

The next witness called is Mr. Patrick. He says, I am a Potter, at Vauxhall; the boy, Foreman, lived with me all the time I have been in the pottery business; that is, between five and six years. He slept in my house only occasionally, and that was whenever I went out of town. As there was no other male in the house on those occasions, he used to sleep there for the purpose of giving the key to the Potter in the morning. I was absent from home on the 25th of September; and on that occasion the Boy slept in my house; he slept upon a chair bed in the front parlour; it was a temporary bed for a nurse occasionally. I knew the Defendant, John Church; I first became acquainted with him when I came to reside at Vauxhall; he is a Baptist Preacher, and I attended his chapel; and that was the way I became acquainted with him. His residence is adjoining to the Chapel. In the month of September, the Defendant came to sleep at my house. He complained occasionally of ill health; and thinking that he was ill, I asked him, out of friendship, to take a bed at my house, as I thought the air would be of service to him. I returned home on the evening of the 26th of September, and on the morning of the 27th the Boy made a communication to me respecting this transaction.

So that you see, Gentlemen, the Boy makes this communication to his master at the earliest moment he has an opportunity of speaking to him.

"Several of the congregation afterwards applied to me, and at their request I went to Mr. Church on the 9th of October."

But, Gentlemen, the 9th of October is not the first time that this matter was mentioned; for it appears to have been in circulation at the time that Mr. Church wrote the letter which has been given in evidence.

"That was the first communication I had with Mr. Church on the subject. Church said he took it extremely kind of me in calling upon him. I said he might take it as he pleased, as I did not come willingly, but that some of his congregation thought that I ought to see him on the business."

You observe, Gentlemen, that it was at the request of some of the congregation that he went; and, in a subsequent part of the evidence, it appears that Mr. Thomas, one of the congregation, had expressly desired him to call upon the Defendant.

"I told him, I waited upon him, having seen a letter, wherein he denied three particular points in the Boy's statement. He then denied, in the fleet place, having taken hold of the Boy, and in the second, his having said to the Boy that he was his mistress. The third point I didn't particularly recollect; but in the course of conversation he admitted that he had been in the Boy's room. He denied that he had had hold of the Boy, and that he had told the Boy that he was his mistress. I told him that of these two points the Boy was positive, and I had no reason to doubt any thing that he said. The Defendant said 'that he was very sorry for it; the worst of it was, it confirmed ancient reports.'"

Gentlemen, this is the language of Church himself. What those antient reports were we have not heard; we are only left to guess at what the expression alluded to.

Upon which Mr. Patrick said, "It did so, and of course," says he, "I told him that I should believe all that I had heard heretofore: and I wished him a good morning. I have never spoken to him since; but I have seen him.—This is an exact copy of the letter dated the 6th of October, addressed to Mrs. Hunter."

Gentlemen, this letter is afterwards read in evidence. Mrs. Hunter being called as a witness, she stated that she believed, from the knowledge that she had of the character of the Defendant's hand-writing, she believes the original from which this copy is taken, was written by him; and Mr. Patrick swears that the letter from which he took this copy was, in his belief, in "the hand-writing of the Defendant."

Now, Gentlemen, upon reading this letter, one is very much struck, not by what it contains, absurd as it is in some respects, and containing something like a profane use of the sacred name of the Saviour, but at the absence of what one certainly might naturally expect to find in the letter of a person writing to a friend, and one of his own congregation, upon this subject. What is so natural as that he should most explicitly and peremptorily deny the whole accusation and charge, and rest with confidence upon his own innocence and the character which he bore amongst his congregation. But instead of that, he envelopes the matter in a sanctified discussion, such as has been read to you, dwelling upon the sacred name of our Saviour in a very indecent manner. I shall read this letter to you again; and if you find any thing in it which can be construed into an express denial of the circumstances charged against him, I am sure it will make a proper impression upon your minds. I confess I can find no such denial. He says, "I am able to contradict three things"—one of which is laying hold of the boy's person, and the other the speaking of his mistress. The third point, Mr. Patrick does not recollect. But, you will observe, he did not deny being in the room: that seems to be a fact now undisputed. The letter is in these words:—

> *Oct.* 6, 1816.
>
> "Dear Mrs. Hunter—My heart is already too much affected. Your letter only added affliction to my bonds; but I forbear. I would have called on you this morning, but I was too low in mind to speak to any friend but Jesus. There I am truly comfortable. Pardon me. But I make no remarks on what you have been told. I must bear it. Though I am able to contradict these things, I would rather not. Mr. and Mrs. Patrick have always dealt kindly to me. I am only grieved that dear Mrs. P. whom I really love, that she should try to injure me in the estimation of those who are real friends to my dear children. The thought affects me, Why hurt my poor family? But I am too much depressed to enlarge. I shall never forget their kindness. God will reward them, as he has many who have dealt well to me. But he will resent cruelty in those who have and are still trying to degrade me. Mrs. P. will live to see it. Dear Mrs. Hunter, I am grieved at heart. I can not relieve your mind. I am truly sorry to lose you as a hearer, because your soul has been blessed, and you know both the plague of the heart and the value of Jesus. May he be increasingly precious to you!—in his person, love, and grave. Farewell, my dear kind friend. The Lord Jesus will reward you for your love to me and kindness to mine. God is not unrighteous to forget your work of faith and labour of love. With many tears I write this. May we meet in glory, when no enemy shall distress my mind, nor sin, nor death shall part us more. I need not remind my dear friend that I am a child of peculiar Providence."

This is very extraordinary. Whether he considers himself as privileged above the rest of mankind, I know not: but it should seem that he does. He says:

> "I am a child of peculiar providence: and that Heart of Eternal Love, and that Arm of Invincible Power, has protected me—has called me to himself—and for every act of straying, will correct me."

Therefore, he admits that he is subject to the punishment of the Divine Being. Whether he is exempt from the temporal jurisdiction for his crimes or not, seems to be a matter of doubt with him: for he says,—

> "In every act of straying, God will correct me with his own hand; but will resent every other hand sooner or later."

So that he admits that for his offences, or his "acts of straying," as he is pleased to call them, God will punish him with his own hand; but that no other hand will punish him. The letter concludes—

> "This you will live to see. Adieu, dear friend: accept the starting tear, and the best wishes of an heart sincere.
>
> "Your's, truly,
>
> "Till we shall meet above."

Gentlemen, this is his letter. If it had been a full and explicit denial of the whole charge, it would have been more favourable to him. One is sorry to see the name of the Divine Being mixed up with so indecent and abominable a story.

Mr. Patrick goes on to state that he denied having had hold of the boy, but he admitted that he was in the room; upon his saying to the Defendant that as to the two points in question, the boy was positive, and that he had no reason to doubt any thing that the boy said, the defendant replied that he was sorry for it, because it confirmed ancient reports. The witness said, "it did so;" and he told him that he should now believe all that he had heard heretofore, and he wished him a good morning. He says, "I never saw him afterwards to speak to him. This is an exact copy of the letter dated 6th October, 1816, addressed to Mrs. Hunter. I took an exact copy of it myself. I did not read the copy of the letter to the Defendant, for I had not the copy with me at that time. With respect to the letter I told him that I wished to know what the three things were that he could deny. I do not recollect the third point; it is not material, he admitted being in the room, but denied the laying hold."

He is asked in what terms the Defendant admitted that he was in the room, and he said the Defendant said, "I was in the room, but I did not lay hold of the boy." He did not say why he was in the room. "I returned the letter of the 6th of October to Mrs. Hunter, from whom I received it."

On his cross-examination he says:—"I mean to say that the Defendant said distinctly that he was in the room. I never said to any person after I had seen Mr. Church that I thought he was not implicated at all in the charge. I gave a person named *Thomas* an account of the conversation I had with the Defendant, but I never accompanied that account with the observation "he is not implicated"—nor to any person. Mr. Thomas went with me to Mr. Church's house, but he did not go in. Mr. Thomas is not a friend of mine. Mr. Thomas walked with me to the door. It was his wife's wish and my wife's that I should make the application to the Defendant. Mr. Thomas walked with me as far as the door of the Defendant, but he did not go in. After I came out from Mr. Church's I had some conversation with Mr. Thomas, and I told him partly what had transpired. It was very short what did transpire. I think I told Mr. Thomas that the Defendant admitted his having been in the boy's room, but I am not very positive as to that point. I know I told him that Mr. Church said he did not lay hold of him. I never made any such answer to Mr. Thomas as that I thought Mr. Church was not at all implicated"—nor any thing conveying that meaning. I never told him directly or indirectly that there was nothing to implicate Mr. Church. I never told Mr. Thomas or any other person that I would prosecute Mr. Church for this crime, because he had said disrespectful things of my wife: but I think I told Mr. I would prosecute the Defendant for the defamation of my wife's character. But this was a considerable time after the transaction in question. I think I did inform Mr. Thomas that I would prosecute the Defendant for the defamation of my wife's character.

The next witness called is Mrs. Hunter, and she says—"I am one of the congregation and a hearer of Mr. Church. I received a letter, dated the 6th of October, but it had no name subscribed to it. I cannot tell from whom it came. It had no place of abode or signature, except the day of the month. I put that letter into the hands of Mr. Patrick, at least I gave it to Mr. Patrick's daughter, who gave it to her father. That letter was returned to me, but I took no further notice of it. After the letter was returned to me, I put it into a drawer, and I do not know what is become of it. I looked for it on the Thursday morning before I came here, but I was unable to find it. I searched diligently for it, but I could find no trace of it."

Under such circumstances, Gentlemen, the original letter having been searched for, and not being to be found, that, in point of law, lets in the copy of it, which could not be admitted as evidence as it existed. She is then asked whether the letter received was in the hand writing of Mr. Church? and she says, "I have seen his writing. I have seen him write in different hands. He does not write always the same. I don't mean to say exactly that he wrote in different hands; but there was such a difference in the same hand-writing that one would hardly think it was the same. I rather think that letter was in Mr. Church's hand-writing, but I could not be positive as there was no name to it. I cannot say positively whether it was or was not his hand-writing. I believed then it was his hand-writing, and I still believe the same. I did not communicate the letter to any body but Mr. Patrick, and I told him that I had received a letter from Mr. Church. The search I made for the letter was last Thursday. I know nothing of it, and I have no reason to believe that it is now in existence. I did not leave a drawer or a place unsearched."

Mr. Patrick is again called, and says that he knew the hand writing of the Defendant in October last. "I copied this letter from the letter I had from Mrs. Hunter. I believe that the letter from which I made this copy was in Mr. Church's hand writing."

Gentlemen you have had that letter read to you; and this is the Case on the part of the Prosecution.

On the part of the Defendant, Gentlemen, it is observed as matter of surprise that the Prosecutor's Counsel have not called the female servant as a witness. It is very true she was not called, but it was open to the Defendant to have called her, and undoubtedly if his Counsel thought that any examination of hers would have been beneficial to him, we must presume that she would have been called. The Bed-room door of the servants, it is observed, was ajar; and it is contended that one of the servants might have been the person who went down stairs to the young man's room: and it is further contended that there was such a deficiency of light that it was impossible for the Prosecutor to identify with certainty the person who entered his apartment. Now whether there is any thing in the observation as to the deficiency of the light, it for you to judge; but this remark fairly arises from the circumstance of the maid's Bed-room door being a-jar. It is most likely that if either of them came out of the room for any improper purpose, she would have shut the door after her: and it is to be recollected that one of the servants was the Boy's own Sister. It is observed likewise as matter of surprise, that Mrs. Patrick is not called. Gentlemen, it would be very disrespectful to Mrs. Patrick to put such a question to her, as whether she offered these indecencies to the Boy; but if the Defendant's Counsel thought that she could not have stood that examination, as I have repeatedly told you, they might have called her.

On the part of the defendant, they called Mr. Thomas, and he says, "I live in Prospect Place, West Square, St. George's Fields. I am by business, an appraiser and undertaker. I know the defendant Mr. Church. I was one of his hearers. I was acquainted with Mr. Patrick, but not until the report was made respecting Mr. Church. I can't say that I have ever seen him attending Mr. Church, as one of the congregation. I went with Mr. Patrick the day he went to Mr. Church's house. It was the 9th of October, a few days after the report. I did not go into the house with him. I stood outside the door. I learned from Mr. Patrick, that he was going to Mr. Church upon the subject of this business. He told me he had a letter of Mr. Church's, and was going to him to make inquiries. He called upon me at my house too with him, and he told me he was going upon the business of this inquiry. Indeed, it was at my request that he should."

So that you see, Gentlemen, it was not the voluntary intrusion of Mr. Patrick upon Mr. Church, when he went to his house; but it is in compliance with the request of some of the Congregation. He says "Mrs. Thomas went to speak to his wife, and it was at my wife's and his wife's request that he went.—The interview with Mr. Church lasted near an hour. It seemed to be a long while, not much less than an hour, as near as I can guess the time. When he came out I put some questions to him respecting what had passed between him and Mr. Church:—I asked him what Mr. Church had said? and he replied that Mr. Church did not say anything."

Now, Gentlemen, it is impossible that Church could have said nothing, for it is not very likely that Mr. Patrick would be occupied for an hour hearing himself.

"He said Mr. Church seemed very much confounded on account of the cause, but said noting."

Certainly, Mr. Thomas, from the nature of things, must be incorrect, for it is impossible that Mr. Patrick could be an hour in conversation with Mr. Church, and that the latter should say nothing. Mr. Patrick could not be an hour in conversation with himself.

"He said Mr. Church seemed very much confounded on account of the cause. He (Patrick) seemed to insinuate that it would be injurious to the cause God. He did not say, "the cause," but I only suppose he meant the cause of God. I asked whether Church had said any thing, and Patrick said "No." He said he seemed very much confused. I said, what do you mean? If there is any thing against the man, do you think I would not have been faithful to him and have charged him with it? Mr. Patrick said, he did not know any thing about that, and that he was not the proper person. He said, "I don't know,—I am not so proper as you." I said to him, "what did he say respecting the report?" He said it was false.—Patrick himself said the report was false. I then said, "what did Mr. Church state respecting its having been reported that he was in liquor?" Mr. Patrick replied, "that that was false, and that there had been a great deal of exaggeration. I never put the question to Mr. Patrick, "whether he thought that Church was implicated in the transaction or not?" I never used these words or any to the same effect. I put these words to him, "Why," says I, "You did nothing. Did Mr. Church acknowledge nothing to you?" "No, Sir," says he, "he did not." I said, "as you can bring nothing against him, let us pray for him, if he was under any such temptation."

The phrase which the witness uses seems to signify that the Defendant's disposition was not very proper. What occasion was there to pray for him not to be guilty of such an offence? What temptation could there be to a moral man to excite him to the commission of so unnatural a crime?

"Mr. Patrick never delivered any opinion to me, whether he thought Church was implicated in the transaction or not. Nothing more passed at the meeting."

On his cross-examination he said, "I heard of this business two or three days after it happened. My wife and I were desirous that Mr. Patrick should go to Mr. Church's. Mr. Patrick brought the boy to me, in order to have him brought face to face with Mr. Church. Mr. Patrick said that the boy was outside. He did not particularly wish me to see the boy; but I certainly supposed that he brought the boy for the purpose of going to Mr. Church's house. Mr. Patrick and I went together, and the boy followed. The boy did not go in with Mr. Patrick. He staid outside the door. He walked on the other side of the way. He waited whilst I waited. We both waited outside."

Now, gentlemen, there is something in the manner in which this person gave his evidence, which leads me to conclude that he has not given a correct representation of all that had passed between him and Mr. Patrick; in the first place he says, that Mr. Patrick told him that Mr. Church now said nothing. Now that is most extraordinary. Can it be believed that Mr. Church had said nothing, or that Patrick had told the witness so? Well, then, as to the rest of his conduct, Mr. Patrick had brought the source of his own information, namely the boy, to the witness, in order that the person who brought forward the accusation might by examined by Mr. Thomas himself, if he chose to inquire into the subject. Mr. Patrick brought him to go to Mr. Church's, and the boy and Mr. Thomas were left outside the door; for he says, "He and I waited outside of the door:" but Mr. Thomas never thinks it worth his while to ask the boy a single question. He never troubles himself to examine into the extent of the charge, or inquire into the foundation of it. But he says, "Mr. Patrick was to go in and learn what Mr. Church said; and then the boy and I were to go in too. Mr. Patrick took the boy with him, in order that he might be taken in to see Mr. Church face to face. He brought the boy with him, and I suppose that was his intention. I declined introducing the boy to Mr. Church, because I had no particular acquaintance with Mr. Church. I was only one of his hearers; and I thought it was too great a liberty for me to speak to him upon the subject. Mr. Patrick wanted me to go into Mr. Church first."

Why, Gentlemen, who was more proper to inquire into such a subject, than a person who attended the defendant in the celebration of divine worship? But Mr. Thomas says, he thought it would be an obtrusion for him to go into Mr. Church's house. What obtrusion could it be in a case of such momentous consequence, where the character and honour of his spiritual teacher were at stake? Why send Mr. Patrick if it was an obtrusion, and if the matter was of so delicate a nature?

Well,—he goes on to say, "I suppose the purpose of bringing the boy was, that he should be introduced to Mr. Church—I have no doubt about it. I don't know any other reason for his being brought—I don't know that Mr. Patrick said that was his reason. I don't know that he said any thing about inviting me to go to with the boy—I don't recollect that he did. I don't remember declining to go in with Mr. Patrick. I had told him that I had no particular interest in the business. I had no more intimacy with Mr. Church except hearing him—I thought that being only a hearer, my visit would be obtrusive. I had no particular interest in the affair, and therefore I declined going in, or taking the boy with me. I saw no necessity, if the defendant did not acknowledge himself guilty of any thing bad. Though the boy was there, I had not the curiosity to examine him, it being a delicate subject. I did not see the importance of coming at the truth of the case, as Mr. Church did not confess any thing; but if Mr. Church had confessed any thing, I should have thought it my duty to take the boy in, and have them face to face."

This, Gentlemen, is a most extraordinary account which Mr. Thomas gives of himself. If he found Mr. Church guilty, he would have confronted the boy with him! But if he denied his guilt, he would not think it necessary to examine the boy! One would have thought that a sense of justice to the defendant, in such a case, would have prompted him to enquire whether the charge was not founded in malice. But no; with the opportunity of questioning the boy on the spot, he leaves the matter untouched.

He says, "When Mr. Patrick came out and said that Mr. Church did not acknowledge any thing of it, he did not think it necessary then to have the boy in." He says, "I never spoke to the boy; I never asked Mr. Patrick, nor did he give any opinion about whether Mr. Church was implicated in the transaction; but in answer to particular parts of the transaction, he said Mr. Church asserted that it was false. I never saw the letter sent to Mrs. Hunter about the three points of denial."

The next witness called is James Reeves; and he says, "I was the Clerk attending the Magistrate when this charge was made at Union Hall. The Magistrate was Mr. Serjeant Sellon. The examination took place on the 19th November. This being a charge of misdemeanour, no account was committed to writing of what the witnesses said. It was merely an entry of the names of the parties and the result. In the first instance, the depositions were taken down upon which the warrant was granted, but I had no instructions to bring the book in which that examination appears. There was an examination afterwards, when the defendant was ordered to find bail, but the evidence was not then taken down."

Mr. Wood is the last witness, and he says, "I was present at the examination of Church before the magistrate, I am a hatter near the Elephant and Castle. I did not take down the testimony of the witness in writing. Freemantle's boy said that he went into the Pottery and told the Potter that there were thieves in the house; and the Potter and he came to search the house. He was asked by Mr. Sellon whether or no he searched the room where Mr. Church slept, and he said no, he did not search that room. Mr. Sellon said "why not search the room?" and the answer he gave was "that the Potter wished to break the door open." Mr. Sellon said "did you try the door to see whether it was open before you talked of breaking it open?" he said "no, he did not wish to disturb his Mistress." I cannot charge my memory whether, whilst the Potter was examined, he said any thing about what the alarm was, that the boy Foreman gave him."

Now, gentlemen, this is the whole of the evidence on both sides, if you don't find any material inroad in the examination of either the boy or Mr. Patrick, you will have to say whether the Defendant be or be not guilty, upon their evidence you will have to say whether you believe the boy's statement, which is in substance this,—that when he was asleep he was awakened by the indecent application to his person and his private parts, of some person's hand, who said, in a feigned female voice, "Adam don't you know me, I am your Mistress." The boy swears most positively that the voice was that of the defendant, and he also swears to his person,—taking this along with you, that there was no other male in the house. The point for your consideration is, supposing this attack to be made upon his person, was it made with the abominable intention charged in this Indictment? If you are of opinion that the person who made this attempt made it with an intention to commit the crime alledged, then the next question for your consideration is,—was it made by the defendant Mr. Church? The prosecutor says, that he had an opportunity of observing the person who entered the room: he was a man of the defendant's size; it was not the person of Mrs. Patrick nor of the maid, and there was no other man in the house. The other material evidence is, that of Mr. Patrick, who states the communication which he had with the defendant—he says, the defendant contradicted three particulars of the boy's statement: but, the contradiction does not go to the fact of his having been in the room. He admits that he was in the room. Then if he was in the room for what purpose was he there? What excuse is there to be found for his being in the room? If he was in that room, for what other object could he be there than that which this boy states?—Can you suppose that the boy's story is the mere invention of his own brain, or the creature of his own imagination? If you find the fact admitted on all hands, that the defendant was there, for what earthly purpose could he be there, than that imputed to him? Gentlemen, the whole is for your consideration. I have no doubt you have paid great attention to the proofs both on the part of the prosecution and that of the defence. You will lay your heads together, and I am persuaded, you will pronounce that verdict, which your conscience dictates, and the evidence requires.

The Jury immediately found the Defendant GUILTY.

Milton Keynes UK
Ingram Content Group UK Ltd.
UKHW030743071024
449371UK00006B/599